KETO RICE COOKER COOKBOOK

101 Ketogenic Recipes Compatible With Aroma, Dash & Most Popular Food Steamers!

BY
KRISTIN AMBER

HEALTHY HAPPY FOODIE PRESS
SAN FRANCISCO, CA

First published 2022

Editor: HHF Press

Art Direction: HHF Press

Illustrations: HHF Press

All photographs in this book © HHF Press or © Depositphotos.com

Published in the United States of America by HHF Press

268 Bush St, #3042

San Francisco, CA 94104 USA

www.HHFPress.com

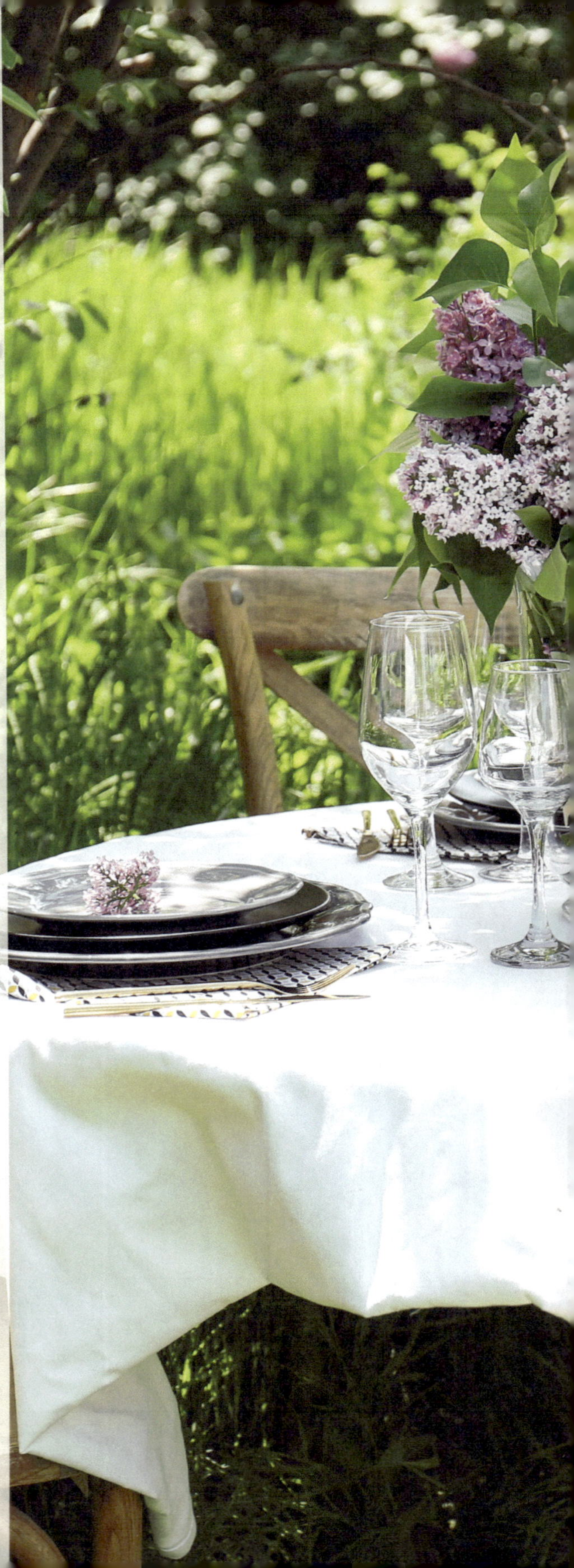

Bon Appétit!

Reader Reviews

Excellent collection of recipes! The "quick start" instructions were very easy to follow, I literally was able to start within 10 minutes as advertised. Straightforward, easy to read, great collection of recipes...this book's a winner.

Samantha S.

The recipes are delicious! This is by far the best cookbook I own. The content flows very logically, starting with "what does it do" and ending with easy and clear instructions on how to get started in just a few minutes. I had no idea my Aroma Rice Cooker was so versatile.

Ron W.

This book is a great companion to the Aroma Rice Cooker. It was clearly written for people who own the Aroma Rice Cooker and the recipes are adapted to it. I LOVE the Keto Southwest steak bowl and the Blueberry Mug Cake!

Brenda A.

For a newbie to Ketogenic food and the Aroma Rice Cooker, this book knocked it out of the park. The contents are well suited to my diet needs and the illustrations and explanations make clear sense. Beautiful book too! Nice layout, awesome exciting design. I loved reading it and using it to create delicious meals!

Dave B.

Wow, I loved how the recipes in this book made me forget I was eating Keto! I mean, we've all seen how dismal Keto food can be...but the recipes I've tried in this book are tasty, exciting, and made me just want to make more and more...

Janice B.

Introduction

WHO THIS BOOK IS FOR

If you have just purchased, or already own, the Aroma Rice Cooker, then you need this book! Here's why:

Get the Most Out of Your Rice Cooker!

Illustrated instructions, a quick start guide and beyond-the-manual tips and tricks will teach you how to get the most out of your grill so that it becomes your family's favorite way to cook rice, steam meats and vegetables, and make healthy soups, stews and much more.

Get a Fast Start With "10 Minute Quick-Start"

Our illustrated "10 Minute Quick-Start" chapter will walk you through your first complete meal in under 10 minutes, so you can quickly enjoy delicious rice, meat, vegetables, and fun things like soups and chili, and more instead of spending all of your time reading instruction manuals.

Clear, Illustrated Instructions

Will make using the Aroma Rice Cooker so simple you can start cooking in minutes while avoiding beginner mistakes such as wrong settings, wrong timing, etc.

Go Beyond the Instruction Manual

Our Pro tips will have you cooking like the pro's in no time. Learn the science behind perfectly steamed rice so that you can confidently make the best, most nutritious meals you've ever had.

Unbiased Recommendations, Workarounds, and Pro Tips

To help you confidently make amazing meals that are perfectly tailored to your family, while avoiding common mistakes, wherever you go!

All the Recipes You'll Ever Need!

101 of the best recipes on the planet will allow you to make the classic breakfasts, lunches, and dinners you are already familiar with, as well as fun and exciting recipes which will give your family the variety they love.

Contents

Main Dishes: Chicken 69

Main Dishes: Beef and Pork 87

Main Dishes: Seafood 105

Desserts 123

AROMA
white rice
brown rice
keep warm
steam
cooking
delay timer
flash rice

CHAPTER 1

About Rice Cookers

What Does it Do?

The Aroma Rice Cooker is a state of the art steaming marvel that allows you to effortlessly cook restaurant quality rice as well as steamed meats, vegetables and complete meals. Finally, you can take all of the guesswork out of achieving perfectly fluffy rice that isn't mushy or too hard. You can also use it as a versatile steamer for meat, fish, and vegetables. And you can use it as a slow cooker for rich, hearty meals like stews, chilis, jambalaya, and so much more.

The Aroma Rice Cooker is designed to be the most durable and reliable rice cooker on the market because it is made from the highest quality materials. This electric cooker requires no additional heat source, and produces perfectly even steam heat for amazingly consistent meals every time you use it. And the Aroma features simple controls that allow you to tailor the cooking process to exactly what you are cooking. Because the Aroma has been designed to produce optimal results for different types of food, you can be sure to always have the fluffiest, most perfectly cooked rice, as well as tender vegetables and meats at the touch of a button.

Have fresh, delicious complete meals waiting for you when you get home. With the easy to use delay timer, you can put all of your ingredients in the cooker and set a timer that will start whenever you want. This way, you can always have the freshest rice without having to wait.

Let's face it, there are a lot of cooking gadgets out there, and chances are you own quite a few. But what if you could combine several cooking appliances into one? By combing a rice cooker, slow cooker, and steamer, you can use one appliance to cook a multitude

of different dishes. Clear out some space in your kitchen while giving yourself all the functionality you need to create the dishes your family loves.

Who Is It Good For?

Because it allows you to make large volumes of rice in one batch, the Aroma Rice Cooker is perfect for families who enjoy fresh, fluffy rice with their meals. Now, you don't have to deal with the inconsistencies of stove top rice cooking which often results in mushy, starchy rice, or rice that feels slightly too hard in the center. The Aroma Rice Cooker allows you to easily cook rice just like at your favorite restaurants.

The Aroma Rice Cooker is perfect for people who want to be able to cook healthy yet delicious meals which are perfectly and tenderly steamed. Rather than cooking with oils and butter, use the Aroma Rice Cooker to make healthy meals the entire family will love, and because you can cook rice and steam a variety of other foods at the same time, you can make a complete meal in no time.

Who Is It NOT Good For?

While you don't have to make large batches of rice with the Aroma Rice Cooker, it does require that you make at least two cups of rice. So if you find that you never need this much rice, the Aroma may be too large for your needs.

A Few Cautions

When cooking with the Aroma Rice Cooker, the inner pot which holds the rice will become quite hot. Always make sure to use oven mitts when removing the inner pot from the rice cooker after cooking, and make sure not to touch the pot while it is still hot. Additionally, allow all of the parts of the rice cooker to cool before touching.

While the Aroma Rice Cooker is a very safe appliance to use, you will want to exercise caution when opening the lid after cooking has finished. Because the Aroma uses steam to cook, a significant amount of steam will be released when the lid is opened. Always make sure to keep your hands and face away from the lid when opening to prevent the possibility of burns.

What Are Its Health Benefits?

Most methods of cooking require some type of cooking fat, and even those which are lower in cholesterol and saturated fat still add many calories to your meal. Because the Aroma Rice Cooker only uses steam to cook, you will be able to prepare the cleanest, healthiest meals without the use of added fats. Additionally, many cooking methods remove or destroy vital nutrients that your body needs. What is the point of cooking with healthy ingredients if your cooking method simply removes everything healthy about your ingredients? By using controlled steam heat, the Aroma Rice Cooker allows you to cook meat and vegetables to a perfectly tender consistency without destroying the nutrients.

A Brief History of Rice Cookers

Rice has been a staple food for many different cultures all over the world for thousands of years, but a specific device for cooking rice is actually a fairly recent invention. In 1937 the first rice cooker was invented but it was completely different from what we now think of as a rice cooker. It consisted of a wooden box with two electrodes to provide heat. It wasn't easy to use or very safe. About a decade later, Mitsubishi invented the first consumer grade rice cooker, but it was also difficult to use and required constant monitoring. All in all, it wasn't much better than just cooking rice on the stove. By the Mid 1950s the Toshiba company figured out a model which used indirect heat and was capable of turning itself to "keep warm" mode automatically. Because it was able to make rice with little supervision, it became a popular kitchen appliance across Asia.

Better Than Stove Top Cooking?

If you look at the instructions on most packages of rice, you will find directions for

stove top cooking. That's because this has, traditionally, been the most common method for cooking rice. But is it the best method? The answer is, no. Rice cooked on the stove cooks unevenly because the heat source is located in one spot: the stove burner. As a result, the bottom of the pot is always going to be hotter than any other part. This means you often end up with some mushy rice and some rice that is still undercooked. The Aroma Rice Cooker, on the other hand, infuses the entire batch of rice with steam for perfectly even cooking, resulting in better consistency every time.

Modern Rice Cookers

Over the years, different companies have continued to improve the rice cooker design, adding features which enabled the cookers to keep rice warm for long periods of time and automatically cook different types of rice. Today, the rice cooker is becoming a popular appliance all over the world because it produces the best, most reliable results. And with the Aroma Rice Cooker you have the flexibility to cook so much more than just rice.

CHAPTER 2

How to Use the Aroma Rice Cooker

Setting Up the Aroma

Remove the Aroma from its packaging and remove the inner pot from the rice cooker. Wash the inner pot with soap and water and wipe the steam vent with a damp cloth.

Your Aroma Rice Cooker includes a special measuring cup to measure rice. Always use this measuring cup when adding rice to the rice cooker. Pour in your desired amount of rice, and rinse the rice several times.

Learning the controls

1. Power Button: Turns the rice cooker on and off.
2. White Rice Button: Press this button when you are cooking white rice.
3. Keep Warm Button: Keeps your food warm once it has finished cooking.
4. Delay Timer: This button allows you to set the delay timer and choose the correct amount of time.
5. Flash Rice Button: Use this option when you need to make rice more quickly than with other settings.
6. Steam Button: Press this button to begin the process of steaming food.
7. Brown Rice: This button allows you to cook perfect brown rice.
8. Plus and Minus Buttons: These buttons allow you to choose the amount of time you will cook for.
9. Cooking LED: This LED will be lit when cooking is in progress.

8
AROMA
white rice
brown rice
keep warm
steam
cooking
delay timer
flash rice
2
3
4
7
6
5
1
9

The Cooking Process

Thanks to the Aroma Rice Cooker, you can be sure that anything you cook will come out perfectly every time. This is because the Aroma Rice Cooker uses evenly distributed steam to infuse each grain of rice with just the right amount of water. Since everything gets just the right amount of moisture, you never have to worry about perfectly consistent results.

Once the Aroma is finished steaming, it will keep your food at the correct temperature for up to twelve hours. But the Aroma also includes a handy steamer basket which allows you to cook other foods while you are cooking rice. Simply add the rice and water to the cooker and then place the items you want to steam in the steamer basket. Place the steamer basket into the rice cooker and close the lid. This way, you can make a complete meal simultaneously using one appliance.

Workarounds

The Aroma Rice Cooker is great for all types of rice, but with so many varieties of rice out there, you may find the need to make some small adjustments here and there. With rice like basmati or jasmine rice, you may find that a small amount of rice sticks to the bottom of the pot of the rice cooker. To avoid this, rinse the rice and soak it in the pot for fifteen to twenty minutes prior to cooking. This will allow a very slight softening of the rice which should help avoid sticking during cooking.

If you happen to be making a large meal, you may find that you have run out of spaces in which to cook. If you need to make a dessert like a cake or pudding, you can use the Aroma to add extra functionality to your kitchen. While a conventional oven is the most common way to cook desserts, you can achieve excellent results and save time using the Aroma.

If you need to make rice or vegetables, but you don't have enough time to wait for the Aroma to complete its regular cooking cycle, you can use the Quick Rice function to speed things up. While you won't get rice that is cooked as perfectly as with the white or brown settings, you will get high quality rice cooked in approximately fifteen minutes. Because brown rice typically takes longer to cook and benefits from pre-cooking soaking, it is recommended that you use an additional 1 1/2 cups of water when using the Quick Rice function to cook brown rice. To make this easier, you can use the included measuring cup to add water to the rice cooker. Two cups of water measured in the measuring cup will equal 1 1/2 cups.

10 Minute Quick-Start

Your First Dinner

Since your Aroma Rice Cooker allows you to cook rice as well as other foods at the same time, you can cook a complete dinner all at once. This is perfect for nights when you don't want to use all of your different kitchen gadgets but you still want to make a complete and healthy dinner. We're going to start with a steamed marinated chicken and vegetables with jasmine rice.

1 Collect These Ingredients:

- 6 boneless skinless chicken thighs
- 2 zucchini, cut into rounds
- 1 cup snap peas
- 2 carrots, sliced
- 1/4 cup soy sauce
- 1/4 cup rice wine vinegar
- 1 clove garlic, finely minced
- 2 Aroma measuring cups of jasmine rice
- water

2 Collect These Tools:

- Chef's knife
- Large ziplock bag
- Aroma measuring cup
- Aroma rice spatula

The goal of "10 Minute Quick-Start" is to walk you through making your first meal so you "learn by doing" in under 10 minutes. Once you've had a chance to get familiar with how your rice cooker works, you can begin experimenting with all different types of foods.

1. Chop all vegetables and set aside. Cut the chicken thighs into small chunks and place into the ziplock bag with the soy sauce, rice wine vinegar, and garlic. Allow to marinate for a few minutes.
2. Measure two Aroma Rice Cooker measuring cups of jasmine rice and add to the inner pot of the rice cooker.
3. Rinse the rice and add water to the correct line in the inner pot.
4. Place the steaming basket over the rice and add the vegetables. Place the chunks of chicken over the vegetables, and close the lid.
5. Set the Aroma Rice Cooker to the 'White Rice' setting.
6. When the rice cooker is finished cooking, open the lid and use oven mitts to remove the steaming basket.
7. Use the Aroma rice spatula to fluff the rice. Mix the contents of the steaming basket together and serve on top of your freshly steamed rice.

Congratulations!

You now have a perfectly cooked dinner for the whole family, and you have learned the basics of how to use the Aroma Rice Cooker!

CHAPTER

3

Pro Tips

Cook the Flakiest Fish You Ever Had

Fish dishes are healthy and delicious but fish can be one of the easiest meats to overcook. Many restaurant chefs know that one of the most reliable ways to get perfectly flaky fish is to steam it. This is because the steaming process allows the fish to cook to the correct temperature while maintaining its delicate texture. Direct heat can cause fish to quickly dry out, while poaching can result in a mushy texture. By cooking your fish in the steamer basket, it will be surrounded by steam so it will cook evenly on all sides, but it won't have the chance to overcook.

Rinse Rice For Best Texture

The texture of rice is based on many factors, and some of these factors, like ideal temperature and timing can be controlled by your Aroma Rice Cooker. Another factor, which many people do not know about, is the amount of starch that coats grains of rice. Almost all rice that has been processed is coated in this dust which will affect your finished product if it is not removed. Essentially, what happens is this starch, rich in proteins, mixes with the cooking water and causes the rice to be coated in a slimy film that allows the grains of rice to stick together. If you've tried cooking your rice in a variety of different ways and still found it a bit slimy or mushy, the extra starch is most likely the culprit. The best rice is firm, but not too firm, and the individual grains shouldn't stick together very much. What about sushi rice, you might be asking? After all, sushi rice is designed to stick together. But sushi rice doesn't stick together because of the starch. It sticks together because it has been treated with a mixture of rice vinegar and sugar after cooking. In fact, the starch on sushi rice is supposed to be rinsed completely before cooking, otherwise it becomes slimy. So, before you cook your rice, add it to the cooking pot and rinse it with cold water and drain several times. You will notice the water becomes cloudy when you add it to the rice. For the best possible rice, rinse it until the water in the pot is completely clear.

Cook Perfect Eggs and Frittatas in the Aroma

We've talked a lot about the best ways to cook different types of rice, but your Aroma Rice Cooker can do a lot more than cook rice. Did you know that it's also a great way to cook egg dishes? The shape of the cooker as well as the even steam heat it produces is perfect for creating eggs with a delightfully delicate texture. Hard boiled eggs are cooked to perfection by adding two cups of water to the bottom of the cooking pot and placing the eggs in the steaming basket. Close the lid and cook for ten to fifteen minutes. That's it. Perfectly cooked hard boiled eggs. If you want to make something more challenging like a frittata, all you have to do is scramble four to six eggs in a bowl and pour into the cooking pot. Then add some chopped veggies like peppers or zucchini to the pot. Add a pinch of salt and pepper, close the lid, and cook on the 'White Rice' setting for five to ten minutes. Open the lid and use the spatula to carefully remove the frittata from the pot.

Make Amazing Desserts

In addition to making amazing rice, eggs, vegetable, and so much more, the Aroma Rice Cooker is perfect for making dessert. Because it offers even and moist heat, it is the perfect way to easily make cheesecake. All you have to do is combine all of the ingredients found in a classic cheesecake (cream cheese, eggs, lemon juice, heavy cream, and flour) and add to the cooking pot. Use the 'White Rice' setting to cook for the regular rice cycle and you will have a perfectly textured and richly flavored cheesecake. You can also make amazing chocolate cake and banana bread with the Aroma Rice Cooker. It's as easy as combining your favorite ingredients and lightly oiling the bottom of the cooking pot. For these types of cakes and breads you will most likely need to use two cycles on the 'White Rice' setting in order for the cake to properly set. This is a great way to bake in the summer when it's too hot to use the oven, or when you are making a large meal and you need extra cooking space.

Experiment with Different Types of Rice

We're all familiar with white and brown rice, but there are so many other types of rice out there that you should get to know now that you are cooking rice like the pros. In the short grain family you have sushi rice, which has a delightfully firm yet fluffy texture, and Arborio rice, which is used for risotto. Arborio has a tough center and a soft outer shell that allows for long, slow cooking and creamy yet perfectly al dente texture.

Long grain rice, like basmati from India and Pakistan, and jasmine rice from Thailand, have a drier texture which works well when paired with thick sauces, but they are also fragrant with a slightly floral and popcorn aroma. There is also a wide variety of long grain rice which is more neutral in flavor and aroma and quite versatile and delicious. One of the most versatile types of the long grain rice is Carolina Gold. Considered the grandfather of American long grain rice, Carolina Gold can be used for many different applications because of its neutral flavor and medium starch content.

If you're looking to really spice things up, try cooking the darker rice varieties like wild rice and forbidden rice, also known as emperor's rice because in China it was traditionally reserved only for the Emperor. These darker rices are also rich in nutrients and pair well with spices, mushrooms, and rich meats. Now that you have learned how to get the most out of your Aroma Rice Cooker you can start experimenting with all of the fun and exotic rice varieties for dishes that will delight everyone.

CHAPTER 4

Breakfast

Brown Sugar & Banana
French Toast Casserole

Sweet and decadent, this breakfast treat will fast become a family favorite.

Serves: 6
Prep Time: 15 Minutes
Cook Time: 30 minutes

6 slices French bread
4 bananas
2 tablespoons brown sugar
1/4 cup cream cheese
3 eggs
1/4 cup milk
1 tablespoon white sugar
1 teaspoon vanilla extract
1/2 teaspoon ground cinnamon
2 tablespoons butter
1/4 cup chopped pecans

1. Cut the bread into 3/4 inch cubes and slice the bananas.
2. Place a layer of bread crumbs on the bottom of a casserole dish.
3. Add one layer banana over the bread and sprinkle with brown sugar.
4. Melt the cream cheese in the microwave then spread half of it over the brown sugar.
5. Repeat steps 2 – 4.
6. Add half of pecans on top of the second layer then slice the butter over the pecans.
7. Beat the eggs in a small bowl, then mix in the sugar, vanilla, milk, and cinnamon.
8. Pour the egg mixture over the bread.
9. Place the steam tray in the pot with 3/4 cup water and carefully lower the dish into the pot.
10. Select the 'White Rice' button, then add 5 minutes to the timer.
11. Allow to cool for 5 minutes then remove and top with remaining bananas and nuts before serving.

Nutrition

Calories: 292, Sodium:301 mg, Dietary Fiber: 3 g, Fat: 10.9g, Carbs: 42.2g, Protein: 8.6g.

Avocado Quiche

Broccoli for breakfast? Yes, and it's amazing.

Serves: 6
Prep Time: 10 Minutes
Cook Time: 42 Minutes

- 2 tablespoons avocado oil
- 6 ounces breakfast sausage
- 3 medium broccoli stalks
- 2 garlic cloves
- Salt and pepper to taste
- 6 eggs
- 1/4 cup heavy cream
- 1 cup shredded Monterey Jack cheese
- 1 green onion
- 1 avocado

1. Chop the broccoli stalks, mince the garlic, and thinly slice the avocado and green onion.
2. Turn the pot onto 'White Rice' setting and add the avocado oil and sausage and cook until the sausage is browned.
3. Spray a casserole dish with cooking spray and transfer the sausage to the dish.
4. Add the broccoli, garlic, salt and pepper to the pot and continue cooking until the broccoli softens then transfer to the casserole dish.
5. In a separate bowl, beat the eggs then mix in the cream, cheese, and the onion until well combined.
6. Pour the mixture into the casserole bowl and cover with foil.
7. Add 1 cup of water to the pot and add the casserole dish with the steam tray.
8. Set the pressure to 'White Rice' and cook for 35 minutes.
9. Allow to sit for 10 minutes before releasing pressure.
10. Remove and top with avocado before serving.

Calories: 333, Sodium:395 mg, Dietary Fiber: 3.5 g, Fat: 26.7g, Carbs: 7g, Protein: 18.2g.

Egg Cups to Go

Keep it simple and healthy with this quick and tasty recipe.

Serves: 4
Prep Time: 5 Minutes
Cook Time: 10 Minutes

4 eggs
1 red bell pepper
1/2 yellow onion
1 Roma tomato
1 cup shredded cheddar
1/4 cup half and half
Salt and pepper to taste
2 tablespoons cilantro

1. Dice the vegetables and set them aside.
2. Combine the eggs, vegetables, 1/2 cup cheese, half and half, salt, pepper, and cilantro.
3. Pour the mixture evenly into 4, 1/2 pint jars and cover loosely.
4. Place the jars on a steam tray in the pot and pour in 1 cup of water.
5. Cook on 'White Rice' setting for 5 minutes.
6. Preheat the broiler on the oven.
7. Vent quickly and transfer to a baking sheet.
8. Sprinkle the remaining cheese evenly over each jar and broil for 2 minutes before serving.

Calories: 157, Sodium: 246 mg, Dietary Fiber: 1.2 g, Fat:8.3g, Carbs: 7.4g, Protein: 13.8g.

Cheesy Poblano
Frittata

Add a little flavor to a breakfast classic with poblano peppers.

Serves: 4
Prep Time: 10 Minutes
Cook Time: 30 Minutes

4 eggs
1 cup half and half
1 can diced green poblanos
1/2 teaspoon salt
1/2 teaspoon ground cumin
1 cup Mexican blend shredded cheese

1. Beat the eggs in a medium bowl, then mix in the half and half, poblanos, salt, cumin, and 1/2 cup cheese.
2. Spray a casserole dish with cooking spray and pour the frittata mix.
3. Place the steam tray in the pan with 2 cups of water and place the casserole dish in the pot.
4. Cook on 'White Rice' setting for 20 minutes.
5. Allow to release pressure naturally for 10 minutes before venting.
6. Preheat the broiler and add the remaining cheese to the top of the frittata and broil until 5 minutes or until the cheese is golden brown.

Nutrition

Calories: 273, Sodium: 752 mg, Dietary Fiber: 0.3 g, Fat:21.3g, Carbs: 6.4g, Protein: 14.8g.

Classic
Quiche

Nothing crazy here, but sometimes classic is perfect.

Serves:4
Prep Time: 10 Minutes
Cook Time: 10 Minutes

1 tablespoon coconut oil
1/2 cup spinach
1/2 cup mushrooms
1/4 cup onion
1/4 cup ham
4 eggs
2 tablespoons milk
2 tablespoons ricotta cheese
1/2 cup shredded cheddar
1/4 teaspoon sea salt

1. Tear up the spinach leaves and chop up the mushrooms, onion, and ham.
2. Spray four, 4-ounce ramekins with cooking spray.
3. Melt the coconut oil in a skillet over medium heat.
4. Add the ham and vegetable to the skillet and cook for about 5 minutes.
5. Beat the eggs in a medium bowl and in the remaining ingredients.
6. Mix the ham and vegetables into the eggs.
7. Add a cup of water to the pot and place a steam tray in the pot.
8. Pour the mixture evenly into each ramekin and place it on top of the steam tray.
9. Set to manual pressure and cook for 6 minutes, release pressure immediately and remove.

Calories: 151, Sodium: 392 mg, Dietary Fiber: 0.4 g, Fat: 10.3g, Carbs: 2.8g, Protein: 12g.

Coffee House
Egg Bites

A creamy and flavorful breakfast delight.

Serves: 4
Prep Time: 10 minutes
Cook Time: 18 Minutes

4 Eggs
4 strips bacon
3/4 cup shredded cheddar
1/2 cup cottage cheese
1/4 cup heavy cream
1/2 teaspoon salt

1. Chop the bacon and cook it over medium heat.
2. Evenly distribute the bacon into 4 mason jars.
3. Add the eggs, cheese, cottage cheese, cream and salt to a blender and blend until smooth.
4. Pour the mixture into the mason jars and cover with foil.
5. Place the jars in the pot and cook on steam for 8 minutes.
6. Allow the pressure to release naturally for 10 minutes before removing.

Nutrition

Calories: 254, Sodium: 1038 mg, Dietary Fiber: 0 g, Fat: 17.1g, Carbs: 2.3g, Protein: 21.8g.

Cheddar, Bacon, Egg Balls

Classic ingredients in a different format make for a fun breakfast.

Serves: 4
Prep Time: 10 Minutes
Cook Time: 14 Minutes

9 eggs
1/2 cup heavy cream
1 cup bacon
1/2 cup shredded cheddar
1 teaspoon dried basil
1 teaspoon salt
1/4 teaspoon pepper

1. Chop the bacon and cook in a skillet over medium heat.
2. Beat the eggs in a medium bowl, then mix in the remaining ingredients.
3. Spray eight, 4-ounce ramekins with cooking spray.
4. Add a cup of water to the pot and place a steam tray in the pot.
5. Pour the mixture evenly into each ramekin and place 4 on top of the steam tray.
6. If you have a silicone mold or second steam tray you can add another layer of jars or working in batches.
7. Set to 'Brown Rice' setting and cook for 14 minutes.
8. Allow the pressure to release naturally for 5 minutes.
9. Carefully remove the ramekins, tip them upside down, and the bites should slide right out.

Calories: 244, Sodium: 922 mg, Dietary Fiber: 0 g, Fat: 18.4g, Carbs: 1.6g, Protein: 18g.

Edible
Breakfast Bowl

Gluten free and vegan breakfast option that is quick and filling.

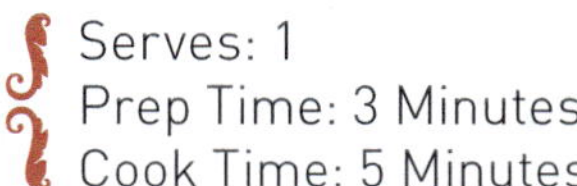

Serves: 1
Prep Time: 3 Minutes
Cook Time: 5 Minutes

1 whole acorn squash
1 container vanilla yogurt
1/2 cup granola
2 tablespoons raw almond butter
2 teaspoons maple syrup
1/4 teaspoon ground cinnamon

1. Cut the squash in half and remove the seeds.
2. Place the steamer basket inside the pot with 1/2 cup water.
3. Place the squash in the basket and steam on manual for 5 minutes.
4. Use a couple of forks to gently transfer the squash halves to a preparation area.
5. Place half of the yogurt in each side of the squash then sprinkle granola over the yogurt.
6. Drizzle the butter and syrup over the granola, then sprinkle on cinnamon before serving.
7.

Calories: 703 Sodium: 207 mg, Dietary Fiber: 20.5 g, Fat: 50.2g, Carbs: 141.3g, Protein: 40.8g.

Family Size Pancake

Imagine a delicious and fluffy pancake, except the size of a cake.

Serves: 4
Prep Time: 5 Minutes
Cook Time: 45 Minutes

2 cups almond flour

2 1/2 teaspoons baking powder

2 tablespoons sugar replacement

2 eggs

1 1/2 cups milk

1. Beat the eggs in a medium bowl, then mix in the milk.
2. Stir in the remaining ingredient to create a thick batter.
3. Coat the bottom of the pot with cooking spray and pour in your batter.
4. Cook on 'Steam' setting for 45 minutes.
5. Press the cake down, it should bounce back, if it doesn't continue cooking on 'Steam' setting for a few more minutes.
6. Use a spatula to loosen the cake from the sides.
7. Flip over and quarter to serve, the top should be perfectly browned.

Nutrition

Calories: 416 Sodium: 97 mg, Dietary Fiber: 6.1g, Fat: 30.7g, Carbs: 18.1g, Protein: 17.8g.

Cherry Chocolate
Oatmeal

Why have bland microwaved oatmeal when you can have this sweet breakfast treat?

Serves: 2
Prep Time: 5 Minutes
Cook Time: 6 Hrs 30 Minutes

- 2 cups oatmeal
- 6 cups water
- 1 cup milk
- 2 1/2 tablespoons cocoa powder
- 1 teaspoon cinnamon
- 1 teaspoon vanilla
- 10 ounce bag frozen cherries
- Cherries and/or chocolate chips for garnish

1. Mix all of the ingredients (minus the garnish) together in the pot.
2. Cook under the 'Steamer' function while vented for 6 1/2 hours.
3. Mix well before transferring to serving bowls.
4. Top with cherries and chocolate chips to serve.

Nutrition

Calories: 638 Sodium: 131 mg, Dietary Fiber: 11.7g, Fat: 12.8g, Carbs: 115.5g, Protein: 17.6g.

Simple
Banana Cinnamon Oatmeal

A quick to make oatmeal that doesn't sacrifice taste for convenience.

Serves: 3
Prep Time: 20 Minutes
Cook Time: 5 Minutes

1 cup old fashioned oatmeal
1 cup milk
1 cup water
2 bananas
2 teaspoons cinnamon
1 tablespoon brown sugar

1. Spray the bottom of your pot with cooking spray and stir in the oatmeal, water, and milk.
2. Thinly slice one of the bananas and stir into the oatmeal along with the cinnamon and brown sugar.
3. Set the machine to 'White Rice' and cook for 5 minutes.
4. Allow the pressure to release naturally for 10 minutes.
5. While the pressure releases thinly slice the second banana.
6. Transfer the oatmeal to serving bowls and top with banana slices before serving.

Calories: 256 Sodium: 42 mg, Dietary Fiber: 6.9g Fat: 3.9g, Carbs: 49.2g, Protein: 8.6g.

Simple
Soy Yogurt

Easy to make, easier to eat.

Serves: 4
Prep Time: 5 Minutes
Cook Time: 14 Hours

32 ounce box plain soy milk
2 tablespoons plain vegan yogurt

1. Divide the milk between 2 pint jars then stir in the yogurt until well blended.
2. Place the jars directly on the bottom of the pan.
3. Set the machine on the 'Yogurt' function for 14 hours.
4. Stir again before serving.

Nutrition

Calories: 207 Sodium: 121 mg, Dietary Fiber: 1.4g, Fat: 8.5g, Carbs: 23.7g, Protein: 9.4g.

Hazelnut Spread Quinoa

Sure, it sounds weird, but it tastes great and is a surprisingly nutritious breakfast.

Serves: 6
Prep Time: 10 Minutes
Cook Time: 10 Minutes

- 1 tablespoon butter
- 1 cup quinoa
- 1 can coconut milk
- 1/3 cup milk
- 1 tablespoon dark cocoa powder
- 1/2 teaspoon hazelnut extract
- 2 tablespoons maple syrup

1. Place the butter in the pot and set the pot to 'White Rice' setting.
2. Add the quinoa and 'White Rice' until it begins to brown.
3. Mix in the remaining ingredients and continue to cook on 'White Rice' setting for another minute.
4. Seal the lid and set the cooker to 'White Rice' setting and cook for 2 minutes once the pressure is reached.
5. Allow to vent naturally for 5 minutes before opening to serve.

Calories: 240 Sodium: 39 mg, Dietary Fiber: 3.2g Fat: 13.6g, Carbs: 26.1g, Protein: 5.6g.

Squash Porridge with Apples

This porridge is healthy and delicious which makes it just right.

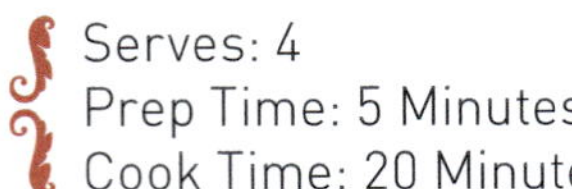

2 large apples
1 delicata squash
1/2 cup bone broth
3 Tablespoons slippery elm
2 Tablespoons gelatin
2 Tablespoons maple syrup
1/2 teaspoon cinnamon
1/8 teaspoon cloves
1/8 teaspoon ginger

1. Core the apple and place the apple and the whole squash into the pot.
2. Pour in the broth and add the cinnamon, cloves, and ginger.
3. Set the pressure to 'White Rice' and cook for 8 minutes.
4. Allow the pressure to release manually for 10 minutes.
5. Remove the squash and cut it in half lengthwise, remove the seeds.
6. Transfer the squash and the contents of the pot to a blender and add the remaining ingredients.
7. Blend until smooth and pour into serving bowls.

Calories: 115 Sodium: 28 mg, Dietary Fiber: 3.1g Fat: 0.2g, Carbs: 22.4g, Protein: 6.1g.

Southwest Breakfast
Casserole

This is a fun and flavorful way to treat the whole family in the morning.

Serves: 3
Prep Time: 10 Minutes
Cook Time: 13 Minutes

4 eggs
2 pounds red potatoes
1/4 yellow onion
1 jalapeño
6 ounces ham steak
1/2 teaspoon salt
1/2 teaspoon mesquite seasoning
1/4 teaspoon chili powder
3/4 teaspoon taco seasoning

1. Dice the onions and jalapeños and cube the ham steak and potatoes.
2. In a medium bowl beat the eggs and mix in the seasonings and salt.
3. Mix in the onions, potatoes or cheese, ham and jalapeño.
4. Transfer the mixture to a greased casserole dish and cover with foil.
5. Place the steam tray in the pot with 1 cup of water then place the dish on top of the steam tray.
6. Set the machine to 'White Rice' setting and cook for 13 minutes, then let pressure release naturally.
7. Serve with tortillas and your favorite breakfast condiments.

Nutritional Info: Calories: 495 Sodium: 1505 mg, Dietary Fiber: 7g Fat: 16.5g, Carbs: 60.3g, Protein: 28.2g.

CHAPTER

5

Soups & Stews

Cheesy Bacon & Cauliflower Soup

If you like cauliflower you will love this rich soup.

Serves: 4
Prep Time: 10 Minutes
Cook Time: 6 Hrs 30 Minutes

2 heads cauliflower
28 ounces chicken broth
21 ounces cheddar cheese soup
1/2 medium yellow onion
2 cloves garlic
1 cup heavy cream
4 tablespoons butter
2 teaspoons xanthan gum
1/2 cup sour cream
8 slices bacon
2 cups shredded cheddar
4 green onions
Salt and pepper to taste

1. Chop the cauliflower, onions, and bacon, and mince the garlic.
2. Combine the cauliflower, yellow onion, soup, broth, garlic, salt, and pepper in the pot and set on 'Steamer Low' setting for 6 hours.
3. Brown the bacon in a skillet over medium heat then set aside and discard drippings.
4. Melt the butter, cream, and xanthan gum together in the skillet until well combined.
5. Mash up any larger pieces of cauliflower.
6. Mix the gum mixture along with 1/2 the bacon, 1 cup cheese, and sour cream, and continue cooking for 30 minutes stirring occasionally.
7. Serve hot and top with remaining cheese, bacon, and green onions.

Nutrition

Calories: 776 Sodium: 4274 mg, Dietary Fiber: 54.6g Fat: 56.1g, Carbs: 72.2g, Protein: 43.9g.

Spiced Cabbage Chicken Soup

A little spice makes this soup perfect for a cold day.

Serves: 10
Prep Time: 10 Minutes
Cook Time: 1 Hr 20 Minutes

- 2 tablespoons olive oil
- 2 pounds chicken breast, boneless, skinless
- 3 cloves garlic
- 1 small cabbage
- 4 ribs celery
- 1 tablespoon curry powder
- 1 tablespoon basil
- 1 1/2 teaspoons sea salt
- 1 teaspoon turmeric
- 1/2 teaspoon ground black pepper
- 1 can coconut cream
- 4 cups chicken bone broth

1. Shred the cabbage, mince the garlic, cube the chicken, and slice the celery ribs into thin slices.
2. Turn the pot to 'White Rice' setting and add the oil, chicken, and garlic and 'White Rice' until the chicken is completely browned.
3. Combine remaining ingredients in the pot and stir well.
4. Set to 'Brown Rice' setting and cook for 20 minutes.
5. Allow the pressure to release naturally and serve while still warm.

Calories: 776 Sodium: 4274 mg, Dietary Fiber: 54.6g Fat: 56.1g, Carbs: 72.2g, Protein: 43.9g.

Simple Vegetable Soup

This recipe is low on carbs and calories, but doesn't sacrifice great taste.

Serves: 12
Prep Time: 10 Minutes
Cook Time: 1 Hr 40 Minutes

1 large turnip
1/4 white onion
6 stalks celery
1 medium carrot
15 ounces pumpkin puree
1 pound frozen green beans
64 ounces vegetable broth
2 cups water
1 1/2 tablespoons basil
1/4 teaspoon thyme leaves
1/8 teaspoon rubbed sage
Salt to taste
1 pound spinach leaves

1. Chop all of the vegetables into bite sized or smaller pieces.
2. Combine all of the ingredients except for the spinach in your pot and set at 'White Rice' setting for 10 minutes.
3. All the pressure to release naturally for 10 minutes.
4. Remove the lid, stir in the spinach, and cover for another 5 minutes.
5. Serve as soon as the spinach is wilted.

Calories: 65 Sodium: 548 mg, Dietary Fiber: 3.8g Fat: 1.2g, Carbs: 9.5g, Protein: 5.5g.

Spanish "Ropa Vieja" Soup

It may literally mean dirty clothes but it offers a fresh flavor profile.

Serves: 10
Prep Time: 5 Minutes
Cook Time: 1 Hr 40 Minutes

- 3 pound chuck roast
- 1 white onion
- 1 clove garlic
- 2 1/2 teaspoons oregano
- 2 teaspoons cumin
- 2 teaspoons paprika
- 2 teaspoons salt
- 1 teaspoon smoked paprika
- 1/2 teaspoon black pepper
- 1/8 teaspoon ground cloves
- 1 can diced tomatoes
- 2 bay leaves
- 2 bell peppers
- Green olives with pimentos

1. Thinly slice the onions and peppers and set them aside.
2. Combine all of the ingredients except for the peppers and olives in the pot and cook on 'Manual' setting for 1 hour and 30 minutes.
3. Allow the pressure to release naturally and shred the roast.
4. Switch the pot to 'White Rice' setting and mix in the peppers, cook for 5 minutes stirring occasionally.
5. Stir in the green olives and serve.

Calories: 314 Sodium: 565 mg, Dietary Fiber: 1.2g Fat: 11.7g, Carbs: 4.3g, Protein: 45.6g.

Buffalo Wing
Soup

Buffalo Chicken is always in because it spicy, salty, and full of flavor. Now you can skip the dips and sauces and spoon it right in.

Serves: 6
Prep Time: 10 Minutes
Cook Time: 20 Minutes

- **1 tablespoon olive oil**
- **1/2 white onion**
- **2 ribs celery**
- **4 cloves garlic**
- **1 pound precooked shredded chicken**
- **4 cups chicken bone broth**
- **3 tablespoons buffalo sauce**
- **6 ounces Cream cheese**
- **1/2 cup half and half**

1. Dice the onion and celery and mince the garlic.
2. Set the pot to 'White Rice' setting and cook the oil, onion, and celery for about 5 minutes or until the celery softens.
3. Add the garlic and cook for another minute.
4. Add the chicken, broth, and buffalo sauce and seal the lid.
5. Press the 'Soup' button then add an additional 5 minutes.
6. Allow the pressure to release naturally for 5 minutes before venting.
7. Scoop out 1 cup of the broth without the chicken and transfer it to a blender.
8. Cube the cream cheese into the blender and puree until smooth.
9. Pour the puree and half and half into pot and stir until mixed evenly then serve.

Nutrition

Calories: 300 Sodium: 905 mg, Dietary Fiber: 0.8g Fat: 16.9g, Carbs: 4.3g, Protein: 30.9g.

Italian Sausage
Soup

This soup tastes so great that you won't even notice that it is missing the carbs.

Serves: 12
Prep Time: 10 Minutes
Cook Time: 20 Minutes

1 pound mild Italian sausage
1 bag whole radishes
1 medium onion
1 clove garlic
32 ounces chicken broth
1/3 cup heavy whipping cream
3 cups kale leaves

1. Mince the garlic and dice the onion and radishes.
2. Set the pot to 'White Rice' and brown the sausage on the bottom of the pot.
3. After the sausage is completely browned, mix in the radish, onion, broth, and garlic.
4. Press the 'Soup' button then add an additional 5 minutes.
5. Allow the pressure to release naturally for 5 minutes before venting.
6. Mix in the kale leaves and cream and cover for 5 minutes to allow the kale leaves to wilt before serving.

Calories: 169 Sodium: 538 mg, Dietary Fiber: 0.9g Fat: 12.4g, Carbs: 4.2g, Protein: 9.7g.

Creamy Broccoli Soup

Skip the calories from the cheddar, but don't sacrifice the flavor.

Serves: 6
Prep Time: 5 Minutes
Cook Time: 15 Minutes

1 tablespoon olive oil
1 white onion
1 pound broccoli
3 medium potatoes
4 cups vegetable stock
2 cloves garlic
1 cup whole milk
1 teaspoon Dijon mustard

1. Chop the onion and broccoli, dice the potatoes, and mince the garlic.
2. Turn the pot to 'White Rice' setting and add the oil and onion.
3. Cook the onions on 'White Rice' setting until they start to turn clear, then mix in the broccoli and potatoes.
4. Pour in the broth and stir well.
5. Seal and cook on 'White Rice' setting for 5 minutes.
6. Allow the pressure to release naturally and mix in the garlic, mustard, and milk.
7. Carefully transfer the mixture to a blender then blend until smooth and serve.

Calories: 157 Sodium: 91 mg, Dietary Fiber: 5.3g Fat: 4.1g, Carbs: 26.3g, Protein: 5.8g.

Basil Tomato Soup

This rich and creamy soup tastes like it came from a 5-star restaurant.

Serves: 8
Prep Time: 15 Minutes
Cook Time: 5 Minutes

1/3 cup olive oil
4 carrots
1 yellow onion
1 tablespoon basil
3 - 28 ounce cans Italian style tomatoes
1 cup chicken broth
1 1/2 cups heavy whipping cream
2 teaspoons Salt
1 teaspoon ground black pepper
2 tablespoons Fresh Basil

1. Peel the carrots, then chop the carrots and onion.
2. Set the pot to 'White Rice' setting and add the oil, onions, carrots, and dried basil to the pot.
3. Cook on 'White Rice' setting for about 5 minutes or until the onions start to turn clear.
4. Stir in the tomatoes, chicken broth, cream, salt, and pepper and seal the pot.
5. Cook on 'White Rice' setting for 5 minutes, then allow to release naturally.
6. While it cooks slice the fresh basil into thin ribbons.
7. Carefully transfer from the pot to a blender and blend until smooth.
8. Top with fresh basil ribbons to serve.

Calories: 175 Sodium: 737 mg, Dietary Fiber: 1.2g Fat: 16.9g, Carbs: 5.5g, Protein: 1.7g.

Taco Soup with Steak

If your mouth isn't watering already, it will be when you smell this soup.

Serves: 6
Prep Time: 5 Minutes
Cook Time: 40 Minutes

2 tablespoons olive oil
2 pounds steak stew meat
1 yellow onion
1 clove garlic
2 bell peppers
12 ounces beef broth
8 ounces Velveeta
1 cup shredded cheddar cheese
1 small can diced tomatoes
2 tablespoons taco seasoning
1/4 cup sliced olives
1/4 cup cilantro

1. Set the pot to 'White Rice' and add the oil and stew meat.
2. Brown the meat on all sides then remove and set aside.
3. Mince the garlic and dice the onion and peppers.
4. Add the onions and garlic to the pot and cook on 'White Rice' setting for about 2 minutes.
5. Add the peppers and cook on 'White Rice' setting for another 5 minutes.
6. Pour a little broth into the pot and scrape up any brown bits from the bottom of the pot.
7. Mix in the remaining broth, meat, cheese, and tomatoes and continue to stir until the cheese is melted evenly through the mixture.
8. Add the taco seasoning and continue to stir until evenly mixed.
9. Seal the pot and cook on 'Soup' mode for 35 minutes.
10. Allow the pressure to release naturally and serve with olives and cilantro for garnish.

Nutrition

Calories: 561 Sodium: 1236 mg, Dietary Fiber: 1.5g Fat: 31.2g, Carbs: 19.7g, Protein: 51.8g.

Asian Pork
Soup

Get your Chinese fix without the carbs usually involved.

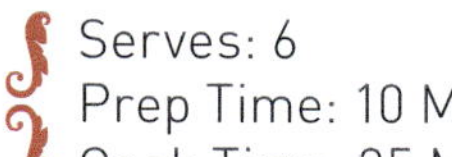

Serves: 6
Prep Time: 10 Minutes
Cook Time: 35 Minutes

- 2 tablespoons soy sauce
- 2 tablespoons black vinegar
- 1 teaspoon sugar
- 2 teaspoons Szechuan peppers
- Salt to taste
- 6 cloves garlic
- 3 inch piece ginger
- 1/2 onion
- 2 tablespoons peanut oil
- 1 pound pork shoulder
- 2 tablespoons doubanjiang paste
- 3 cups water
- 4 cups bok choy
- 1/4 cup cilantro

1. Mince the garlic, ginger, and peppers.
2. Chop the onion and bok choy.
3. Turn the pot to 'White Rice' setting and add the oil, garlic, and ginger to the pot and cook for a few minutes.
4. Stir in the remaining ingredients except for the cilantro and bok choy.
5. Cook on 'White Rice' setting for 20 minutes, then allow the pressure to release naturally for 10 minutes.
6. Stir in the bok choy and cover allowing to cook in residual heat for 10 minutes.
7. Top with cilantro and serve.

Calories: 351 Sodium: 427 mg, Dietary Fiber: 1.6g Fat: 21.1g, Carbs: 20.5g, Protein: 19.9g.

Classic White Chili
with Chicken

This is a satisfying dish that offers a fresh take on boring old chili.

Serves: 8
Prep Time: 5 Minutes
Cook Time: 27 Minutes

1 tablespoon olive oil
2 pounds skinless boneless chicken breast
1/2 yellow onion
1 jalapeño
3 cloves garlic
32 ounces chicken bone broth
2 teaspoons ground cumin
1 teaspoon chili powder
1 teaspoon salt
1/2 teaspoon cayenne pepper
1 bag frozen cauliflower

1. Chop the onion and jalapeño and mince the garlic.
2. Set the pot to 'White Rice' setting and add the oil, chicken, jalapeño, and onions.
3. Brown the chicken lightly, then add the garlic and cook on 'White Rice' setting for another minute.
4. Stir in the broth, cumin, chili powder, salt, and cayenne pepper and seal.
5. Cook on 'White Rice' setting for 10 minutes.
6. Cook the cauliflower, then transfer to a blender and puree.
7. Allow the pressure to release naturally and mix in the cauliflower before serving.

Nutrition

Calories: 264 Sodium: 595 mg, Dietary Fiber: 1g Fat: 10.5g, Carbs: 2.8g, Protein: 37.8g.

Classic Chili
with Tomatillos

A perfect classic chili with tomatillos for a little flair.

Serves: 8
Prep Time: 15 Minutes
Cook Time: 35 Minutes

1 pound ground beef
1 pound ground pork
3 tomatillos
1/2 white onion
6 ounces tomato paste
1 teaspoon garlic powder
1 jalapeño pepper
1 tablespoon ground cumin
1 tablespoon chili powder
1 cup water

1. Chop the tomatillos, jalapeño, and onion.
2. Turn the pot to 'White Rice' setting and brown the beef and pork together.
3. Mix in the remaining ingredients until well blended and seal the pot.
4. Cook on 'White Rice' setting for 35 minutes.

Calories: 218 Sodium: 103 mg, Dietary Fiber: 1.7g Fat: 6.1g, Carbs: 6.6g, Protein: 33.5g.

Chicken Chile Soup

Regular chicken soup can be a bit drab but adding the poblano peppers really kicks it up a notch.

Serves: 6
Prep Time: 5 Minutes
Cook Time: 10 Minutes

4 chicken breasts
1 tablespoon olive oil
2 poblano peppers
1 onion
3 cloves of garlic
1 jalapeño
1 tablespoon cumin
1 small can diced tomatoes
16 ounce jar salsa verde
32 ounce box chicken broth
4 ounces reduced fat cream cheese
1/2 cup light sour cream

1. Chop the poblanos and onions and mince the garlic and jalapeño.
2. Turn the pot to 'White Rice' setting and add the oil and the chicken, sear the chicken until browned on both sides then remove and set aside.
3. Add the vegetables to the pot and stir in the cumin.
4. Add the broth, tomatoes, and salsa and stir evenly, then return the chicken to the pot.
5. Seal the pot and cook on 'White Rice' setting for 5 minutes, then let the pressure release naturally for another 5 minutes.
6. Remove the chicken from the pot and shred it, then return it to the pot.
7. Stir in the sour cream and cream cheese until completely blended and serve.

Nutrition

Calories: 346 Sodium: 1027 mg, Dietary Fiber: 1.5g Fat: 18.5g, Carbs: 11.2g, Protein: 33.9g.

White Bean and Kale
Soup

It may sound bland, but this soup has a great mixture of flavor and texture.

Serves: 8
Prep Time: 10 Minutes
Cook Time: 45 Minutes

- 1 cup dry navy beans
- 2 quarts chicken broth
- 4 cloves garlic
- 1 bay leaf
- 1 cup kale
- 1 tablespoon olive oil
- 2 tablespoons butter
- 1 teaspoon oregano
- 1 tablespoon tomato paste
- 1/2 pound sausage
- Salt and pepper to taste

1. Crush the garlic and chop the kale.
2. Rinse the beans and set aside.
3. Turn the pot to 'White Rice' setting and add the oil and sausage.
4. Brown the sausage, then mix in the remaining ingredients.
5. Seal the pot and turn it to the 'Soup' function and cook for 45 minutes.
6. Allow the pressure to release naturally and serve hot.

Calories: 271 Sodium: 1003 mg, Dietary Fiber: 6.7g Fat: 14.5g, Carbs: 18.7g, Protein: 16.7g.

CHAPTER

6

Pastas & Casseroles

Noodle-less Lasagna

Skip the carbs but not the flavor with this noodle-less Lasagna.

Serves: 8
Prep Time: 25 Minutes
Cook Time: 25 minutes

1 pound ground beef
2 cloves garlic
1 small onion
1 1/2 cups ricotta cheese
1/2 cup parmesan cheese
1 egg
1 jar marinara sauce
9 mozzarella slices

1. Mince the garlic and chop the onion.
2. Turn the pot to 'White Rice' setting and brown the beef with the onion and garlic.
3. Beat the egg in a small bowl and mix in the ricotta and Parmesan.
4. Drain excess fat from the beef mix, then mix in the marinara.
5. Spoon half the meat sauce into a casserole and top with 4 slices of mozzarella.
6. Spread 1/2 the ricotta mix over the mozzarella.
7. Repeat steps 5 and 6 reserving a little meat sauce to top the final layer.
8. Cover the lasagna loosely with foil.
9. Place the steam tray in your pot with one cup of water and place the casserole dish on the steam tray.
10. Seal and cook on 'White Rice' setting for 10 minutes.
11. Allow the pressure to release naturally and serve.

Calories: 305 Sodium: 439 mg, Dietary Fiber: 1g Fat: 14.6g, Carbs: 9g, Protein: 33.5g.

Classic Chicken
Cacciatore

Eat by itself or use it as it was meant over your favorite pasta substitute.

Serves: 4
Prep Time: 10 Minutes
Cook Time: 25 Minutes

1 tablespoon oil
4 bone in chicken thighs
1/2 can crushed tomatoes
1/2 onion
1/2 red bell pepper
1/2 green bell pepper
1/2 teaspoon oregano
1 bay leaf

1. Set the pot to 'White Rice' setting and add the oil.
2. Brown the chicken in the pot on both sides.
3. Dice the onion and bell pepper.
4. Remove the chicken and set aside then add the onion and bell pepper and cook on 'White Rice' setting for about 5 minutes.
5. Return the chicken to the pot and add the rest of the ingredients stir together until the chicken is well coated.
6. Seal the pot and cook on 'White Rice' setting for 25 minutes.
7. Let the pressure release naturally and remove the bay leaf before serving.

Calories: 289 Sodium: 116 mg, Dietary Fiber: 1.2g Fat: 20.5g, Carbs: 4.1g, Protein: 20.7g.

Low-Carb
Pulled Pork Ragu

Serve this delicious sauce over spiralized zucchini or spaghetti squash.

Serves: 10
Prep Time: 15 Minutes
Cook Time: 45 Minutes

18 ounce pork tenderloin
Salt and pepper to taste
1 teaspoon olive oil
5 cloves garlic
1 can crushed tomatoes
1 small jar roasted red peppers
2 sprigs fresh thyme
2 bay leaves

1. Turn the pot to 'White Rice' setting and add the oil.
2. Crush the garlic and add it to the oil to cook.
3. Season the pork with salt and pepper.
4. Remove the garlic with a slotted spoon and add the pork to the pot.
5. Brown the pork on both sides then add the remaining ingredients.
6. Cook on 'White Rice' setting for 45 minutes.
7. Allow the pressure to release naturally and remove the bay leaves before serving.

Nutrition

Calories: 90 Sodium: 82 mg, Dietary Fiber: 0.7g Fat: 2.3g, Carbs: 2.6g, Protein: 13.9g.

Low-Carb Chicken Puttanesca

Enjoy delicious spaghetti alla puttanesca without the carb filled spaghetti.

Serves: 6
Prep Time: 10 Minutes
Cook Time: 15 Minutes

6 chicken thighs
2 tablespoons olive oil
2 cloves garlic
Salt and pepper to taste
1/2 tsp red chili flakes
1 can chopped tomatoes
6 ounces pitted black olives
1 tablespoon capers
1 tablespoon basil

1. Turn the pot to 'White Rice' setting and add the oil.
2. Place the chicken in the oil skin side down and cook until browned.
3. Add in the remaining ingredients to the pot. Mix well.
4. Continue to cook on 'White Rice' setting until the sauce comes to a gentle simmer.
5. Seal the lid and turn the pot to 'White Rice' setting.
6. Cook for 15 minutes then allow the pressure to release naturally for 12 minutes.
7. Serve over spiralized vegetables.

Nutrition

Calories: 357 Sodium: 610 mg, Dietary Fiber: 1.4g Fat: 18.6g, Carbs: 3.4g, Protein: 42.8g.

Stroganoff

Rich and creamy beef stroganoff that won't break your diet.

Serves: 4
Prep Time: 5 Minutes
Cook Time: 30 Minutes

1 tablespoon oil
1/2 onion
1 clove garlic
1 pound beef stew meat
1 1/2 cups mushrooms
1 tablespoon Worcestershire sauce
1 teaspoon salt
1 teaspoon pepper
1/3 cup sour cream
1/4 teaspoon xanthan gum

1. Chop the onion and mince the garlic.
2. Turn the pot to 'White Rice' setting and cook the onion and garlic for a few minutes.
3. Combine the rest of the ingredients except the sour cream and gum in the pot.
4. Seal the pot and cook on 'White Rice' setting for 20 minutes.
5. Allow the pressure to release naturally, then turn the pot back to 'White Rice'.
6. Stir in the sour cream and xanthan gum, shaking in a little at a time.
7. Eat by itself or over cauliflower for a low carb delight.

Calories: 303 Sodium: 921 mg, Dietary Fiber: 7g Fat: 14.6g, Carbs: 10.6g, Protein: 36.6g.

Low Carb Chicken Alfredo
with Spaghetti Squash

The same great chicken alfredo taste without the high-carb noodles.

Serves: 5
Prep Time: 5 Minutes
Cook Time: 35 Minutes

- 1 whole spaghetti squash
- 1 pound boneless, skinless chicken breast
- 4 ounces cream cheese
- 1/2 cup chicken broth
- 2 cups broccoli
- 1 cup shredded Parmesan
- 1/4 cup heavy whipping cream
- 3/4 tablespoons butter
- 1 tablespoon flour
- 1 tablespoon garlic
- 2 cups almond milk
- 1 teaspoon olive oil

1. Cut the squash in half the short way, remove and discard the seeds.
2. Put one cup of water in the pot and place the squash halves inside with the flesh facing up.
3. Seal and cook on 'White Rice' setting for 7 minutes.
4. While the squash cooks, mince the garlic, chop the broccoli, and cube the chicken.
5. Manually release the squash and transfer to a bowl.
6. Use a fork to shred the squash into spaghetti.
7. Pour the water out and return the pot.
8. Turn the pot to 'White Rice' setting and add the oil.
9. Add the chicken and cook until browned all over, then remove and set aside.
10. Add the garlic and continue to cook for another minute.
11. Add the chicken broth and scrape up the brown bits on the bottom.
12. Add in the almond milk, whipping cream, cream cheese, and butter and continue stirring until the ingredients are well combined.
13. Stir in the broccoli and Parmesan and cook until the broccoli softens.
14. Stir in the flour to thicken the sauce.
15. Add the chicken back to the pot and stir in.
16. Serve the sauce over the spaghetti squash.

Nutrition

Calories: 498 Sodium: 289 mg, Dietary Fiber: 3.6g Fat: 39.5g, Carbs: 12.6g, Protein: 27.1g.

Low-Carb Bruschetta
Chicken

Bruschetta is typically an antipasto dish, and is traditionally served on or with toasted bread. But this version is just as delicious and designed for those of us watching our carb intake! Try serving alongside soup or greens for a healthy, tasty treat.

Serves: 6
Prep Time: 10 Minutes
Cook Time: 7 Minutes

2 pounds boneless, skinless chicken breast
1 tablespoon olive oil
1/2 cup chicken broth
Salt and pepper to taste
1 can diced tomatoes
1 teaspoon oregano
4 cloves garlic
1/4 cup balsamic vinegar
1 teaspoon basil

1. Mince the garlic and place in a medium bowl.
2. Mix in the tomatoes, oregano, vinegar, and basil in the bowl.
3. Turn the pot to 'White Rice' setting and add the olive oil.
4. Add the chicken breasts and brown on both sides.
5. Transfer the chicken to a bowl and season with salt and pepper.
6. Add the chicken broth to the pot and scrape up any brown bits that were left behind by the chicken.
7. Pour 1/2 of the tomato sauce into the pot with the chicken and seal the pot.
8. Cook on 'White Rice' setting for 7 minutes, then allow the pressure to release naturally for 5 minutes.
9. Serve your chicken over your favorite noodle substitute and top with the remaining sauce.

Calories: 207 Sodium: 143 mg, Dietary Fiber: 0.5g Fat: 6.3g, Carbs: 2.2g, Protein: 32.9g.

Vegetable Lasagna

This recipe takes a little more work and time than the no noodle lasagna but it's worth it.

Serves: 6
Prep Time: 30 Minutes
Cook Time: 4 Hours

2 zucchinis
1 eggplant
2 cups pasta sauce
1 red onion
1 red bell pepper
16 ounces low-fat cottage cheese
2 eggs
8 ounces part-skim shredded mozzarella

1. Slice the zucchinis and eggplant vertically into thin slices and lay them on a kitchen towel, let stand for 15 minutes.
2. Dice the onion and pepper.
3. Transfer the zucchini to a baking sheet and turn on your broiler.
4. Broil the zucchini for 5 minutes.
5. In a medium bowl beat the eggs then mix in the cottage cheese.
6. Spread 1/2 cup of pasta sauce on the bottom of your pot.
7. On the pasta sauce add a layer of eggplant, 1/3 cottage cheese, 1/3 peppers and onions, 1/3 mozzarella, and 1/2 cup of sauce.
8. Repeat step 7 using zucchini instead of eggplant.
9. Repeat step 7 again with the eggplant.
10. Turn the pot to 'Steamer' function and cook on high for 3 hours.
11. Turn the pot to keep warm and allow to cook another hour before serving.

Calories: 298 Sodium: 946 mg, Dietary Fiber: 6.2g Fat: 12.2g, Carbs: 24.2g, Protein: 23.7g.

Mexican Lasagna
Casserole

A protein packed dish that your family won't even realize is healthy.

Serves: 8
Prep Time: 20 Minutes
Cook Time: 2 Hrs 30 Minutes

- **2 teaspoons olive oil**
- **2 pounds lean ground beef**
- **1 onion**
- **1 tablespoon taco seasoning**
- **1 cup salsa**
- **2 cans tomatoes and green chiles**
- **6 low-carb tortillas**
- **2 cups cottage cheese**
- **2 eggs**
- **3 cups shredded Mexican cheese**

1. Turn the pot to 'White Rice' setting and add the oil.
2. Add the ground beef and cook to brown breaking apart with a spatula as you go.
3. Chop the onion.
4. Push the beef to the side and add the onion and 'White Rice' for a few minutes, then mix it with the beef.
5. Add the salsa, taco seasoning, and cans of tomatoes and chiles and continue to cook until the liquid evaporates.
6. In a bowl mix together the cottage cheese, eggs, and 1 cup of cheese.
7. Turn the machine off, remove the beef mixture and set aside.
8. Cut the tortillas in half.
9. Add half the beef mixture to the pot, then top with half the cottage cheese, a cup of cheese and the tortillas.
10. Add the remaining ingredients in the same order as before.
11. Cover and cook with the 'Steamer' function on high for 2 hours and 30 minutes.

Calories: 488 Sodium: 1112 mg, Dietary Fiber: 7.3g Fat: 19.4g, Carbs: 22.7g, Protein: 53.5g.

Easy Cheeseburger Casserole

You won't have to make a separate meal for the kids with this family friendly dish.

Serves: 10
Prep Time: 20 Minutes
Cook Time: 4 Hours

2 tablespoons olive oil
2 pounds ground beef
1/2 teaspoon salt
1/2 teaspoon pepper
1/2 teaspoon garlic salt
1 can cream of mushroom soup
1 can Cheddar cheese soup
1/2 pound bacon
1/2 onion
2 cups shredded Cheddar cheese

1. Chop the bacon and thinly slice the onion.
2. Turn the pot to 'White Rice' setting and add the oil.
3. Add the bacon and brown it.
4. Add the beef to the pot and brown it.
5. Mix in the salt, pepper, and garlic salt.
6. Mix in the soups until all ingredients are evenly combined.
7. Layer the onions over the mix.
8. Top with the cheese and cover.
9. Turn the machine to the 'Steamer' function and cook on low for 4 hours.

Nutrition

Nutritional Info: Calories: 472 Sodium: 1262 mg, Dietary Fiber: 0.4g Fat: 29.7g, Carbs: 5.8g, Protein: 43.4g.

Cabbage
Casserole

This is a fantastic recipe to fix in the morning and enjoy at night.

Serves: 4
Prep Time: 20 Minutes
Cook Time: 8 Hours

1 1/2 pounds ground beef
1 bag riced cauliflower
1 cabbage
2 cups fresh tomatoes
1 onion
3 cloves garlic
2 teaspoons dried oregano
1 cup tomato sauce
2 cups beef broth
Salt and pepper to taste

1. Slice the cabbage, mince the garlic, and chop the onion and tomatoes.
2. Add the beef, cauliflower, cabbage, tomatoes, onion, and garlic to the pot.
3. Sprinkle salt, pepper, and oregano over the ingredients.
4. Add the tomato sauce and broth and give everything a good stir.
5. Cover and turn the pot to 'Steamer' and cook for 8 hours.

Calories: 435 Sodium: 876 mg, Dietary Fiber: 7.9g Fat: 11.9g, Carbs: 22.7g, Protein: 58.9g.

CHAPTER 7

Main Dishes

Chicken

Spinach and Artichoke
Chicken Breast

This meal has you covered in every category from how good it tastes to how quick and easy it is to make.

Serves: 6
Prep Time: 5 Minutes
Cook Time: 15 Minutes

1 tablespoon olive oil
1 pound boneless, skinless, chicken breast
2 cups spinach
1 can artichoke hearts
4 ounces cream cheese
1/2 cup heavy cream
1/4 cup Parmesan
1/2 Cup shredded mozzarella
1 teaspoon garlic powder
1 teaspoon onion powder
Salt & pepper to taste

1. Cube the chicken and drain and chop the artichokes and spinach.
2. Turn the pot to 'White Rice' setting and add the oil and chicken.
3. Brown the chicken then add the artichokes, garlic powder, onion powder, salt, and pepper and continue cooking for another 3 minutes.
4. Turn the pot to "Keep Warm" and stir in the remaining ingredients.
5. Cover and allow the cheeses to melt stirring every few minutes until blended evenly.

Nutrition

Calories: 227 Sodium: 164 mg, Dietary Fiber: 1.5g Fat: 14.4g, Carbs: 4.2g, Protein: 21.4g.

Chicken in Creamy Salsa

This recipe is proof that you can make amazing meals no matter what you have in your refrigerator.

Serves: 6
Prep Time: 10 Minutes
Cook Time: 20 Minutes

3 pounds boneless, skinless chicken breasts
1/2 cup chicken broth
4 ounces cream cheese
1/2 cup cottage cheese
1 cup salsa
2 teaspoons taco seasoning

1. Combine the chicken and the broth in the pot and seal and cook on the 'Poultry' setting for 10 minutes.
2. Allow the pressure to release naturally and transfer the chicken to a bowl, reserve 1/2 cup of the broth and discard the remaining liquid.
3. Add the broth back to the pot along with the remaining ingredients and switch the pot to 'White Rice' setting.
4. Stir continuously until the ingredients create a smooth sauce.
5. Shred the chicken and return it to the pot on 'Keep Warm' setting.
6. Allow to sit for a few minutes before serving.

Calories: 652 Sodium: 918 mg, Dietary Fiber: 0.7g Fat: 30.8g, Carbs: 12.9g, Protein: 77.6g.

Low Carb
Buffalo Chicken Wraps

The amazing taste of buffalo chicken without the carbs.

Serves: 4
Prep Time: 5 Minutes
Cook Time: 15 Minutes

1 1/4 pounds boneless, skinless chicken breast

2 stalks celery

1 onion

1 medium carrot

1 cup buffalo sauce

12 bib lettuce leaves

1. Dice the carrot, onion, and celery.
2. Combine all of the ingredients except for the lettuce in the pot and mix to coat the chicken.
3. Seal the pot and cook on 'High' setting for 15 minutes.
4. Allow the pressure to release naturally and move the chicken to a bowl.
5. Shred the chicken then return it to the pot and stir it in.
6. Serve the mixture in the lettuce leaves.

Nutrition

Calories: 186 Sodium: 332 mg, Dietary Fiber: 1.5g Fat: 3.6g, Carbs: 5.3g, Protein: 30.6g.

Creamy Crack Chicken

This recipe is so rich and smooth that you won't believe that it is keto friendly.

Serves: 8
Prep Time: 5 Minutes
Cook Time: 20 Minutes

2 slices bacon

2 pounds boneless, skinless chicken breasts

2 blocks cream cheese

2 tablespoons apple cider vinegar

1 tablespoon dried chives

11/2 teaspoons garlic powder

11/2 teaspoons onion powder

1 teaspoon crushed red pepper flakes

1 teaspoon dried dill

1/4 teaspoon salt

1/4 teaspoon black pepper

1/2 cup shredded cheddar

1 scallion

1. Chop the bacon and scallion.
2. Turn the pot to 'White Rice' setting and add the bacon.
3. Cook the bacon until it browns then press cancel to turn the heat off and set the bacon side.
4. Combine the chicken, cream cheese, water, vinegar, chives, garlic powder, onion powder, crushed red pepper flakes, dill, salt, and pepper in the pot and cook on 'White Rice' setting for 15 minutes.
5. Allow the pressure to release naturally and transfer the chicken to a bowl.
6. Shred the chicken then return it to the pot and mix in the cheddar.
7. Top with bacon and chopped scallion before serving.

Calories: 291 Sodium: 350 mg, Dietary Fiber: 0.4g Fat: 13.2g, Carbs: 3.9g, Protein: 37.4g.

Buttery Garlic Chicken

It only takes a few ingredients and less than an hour to make this surprisingly satisfying entrée.

Serves: 4
Prep Time: 5 Minutes
Cook Time: 40 minutes

4 boneless, skinless chicken breasts

1/4 cup turmeric ghee

1 teaspoon salt

10 cloves garlic

1. Dice the garlic then combine the garlic and remaining ingredients in the pot.
2. Seal and cook on 'White Rice' setting for 35 minutes.
3. Manually allow the pressure to release naturally and shred the chicken before serving.

Calories: 312 Sodium: 711 mg, Dietary Fiber: 1.6g Fat: 11.5g, Carbs: 6.8g, Protein: 43.2g.

Whole Chicken
Roast

It doesn't get much easier or simpler than this to feed the family.

Serves: 5
Prep Time: 5 minutes
Cook Time: 35 Minutes

1 teaspoon paprika
1 teaspoon garlic powder
1 teaspoon ginger
1 teaspoon ground coriander
1/4 teaspoon ground nutmeg
Salt and pepper to taste
3 tablespoons olive oil
1 cup chicken broth
3 pound whole chicken

1. Mix together the spices along with 2 tablespoons of olive oil and 2 tablespoons of chicken broth to form a paste.
2. Put the chicken in a bowl and rub the paste over the chicken.
3. Turn the pot to 'White Rice' setting and add the remaining oil.
4. Place the chicken in the pot and brown on all sides.
5. Remove the chicken and set aside.
6. Add the remaining chicken broth to the pot along with the steam tray, then return the chicken to the pot.
7. Set the machine on 'White Rice' setting and cook for 25 Minutes.
8. Allow the pressure to release naturally before removing the chicken to serve.

Nutrition

Calories: 602 Sodium: 387 mg, Dietary Fiber: 0.3g Fat: 29g, Carbs: 1.1g, Protein: 79.9g.

Easy
Curry Chicken

Perfectly spiced chicken that you can feel great about eating.

Serves: 3
Prep Time: 10 Minutes
Cook Time: 40 Minutes

3 frozen chicken breasts
1/2 yellow onion
1/2 teaspoon pure liquid stevia
1/2 teaspoon ground ginger
2 tablespoons garlic powder
2 teaspoons curry powder
2 teaspoons ground cumin
1/4 teaspoons ground cloves
1 tablespoon apple cider vinegar
1 tablespoon lemon juice
1 tablespoon arrowroot powder

1. Dice the onion then add all of the ingredients except the arrowroot in the pot and mix around to coat the chicken.
2. Turn the pot to the 'Meat/Stew' setting, seal and cook for 40 minutes.
3. Manually allow the pressure to release naturally, then transfer chicken to a bowl and shred.
4. Stir the arrowroot powder into the pot to thicken the liquid, then transfer the chicken back to the pot and stir it into the sauce before serving.

Nutrition

Calories: 171 Sodium: 82 mg, Dietary Fiber: 1.7g Fat: 2.2g, Carbs: 10.3g, Protein: 27.6g.

Sweet Chicken Drumsticks

A fun recipe that proves that chicken doesn't have to be boring.

Serves: 4
Prep Time: 5 Minutes
Cook Time: 30 Minutes

1/4 cup low Sodium soy sauce
3 tablespoons rice wine
2 tablespoon honey
2 cloves garlic
1 teaspoon grated ginger
8 skinless chicken drumsticks
1 tablespoon sesame seeds

1. Turn the pot to 'White Rice' setting and add the soy sauce, rice wine, honey, garlic, ginger and 'White Rice' for 2 minutes.
2. Add the chicken to the mix and seal the pot.
3. Cook on high for 20 minutes then allow the pressure to release naturally.
4. Sprinkle the sesame seeds over the chicken and serve.

Calories: 498 Sodium: 906 mg, Dietary Fiber: 0.5g Fat: 25.2g, Carbs: 16.8g, Protein: 47.4g.

Simple Harissa Chicken

Low carb, low calorie chicken with a Moroccan flair.

Serves: 4
Prep Time: 5 Minutes
Cook Time: 20 Minutes

1 pound boneless, skinless chicken breasts

1/2 teaspoon ground cumin

1/4 teaspoon garlic powder

Salt and pepper to taste

1 cup mild Harissa sauce

1. In a small bowl, mix together the cumin, garlic, salt and pepper.
2. Sprinkle the spice mix over both sides of the chicken then transfer the chicken to the pot.
3. Pour the Harissa sauce over the chicken and stir to make sure the chicken is well coated.
4. Cook on 'White Rice' setting for 20 minutes, then allow the pressure to release naturally.
5. Transfer the chicken to a bowl and shred before serving.

Calories: 247 Sodium: 248 mg, Dietary Fiber: 0.1g Fat: 10.4g, Carbs: 4.3g, Protein: 32.9g.

Sweet and Spicy Chicken

The sweetness of coconut mixed with spicy curry creates a flavor delight!

Serves: 4
Prep Time: 5 Minutes
Cook Time: 40 Minutes

1 tablespoon coconut oil
1 yellow onion
3 tablespoons curry powder
2 cloves garlic
1 can diced tomatoes
1 can tomato sauce
1/2 cup chicken broth
2 tablespoons white sugar
2 pounds chicken breasts
Salt and pepper to taste
1 can coconut milk

1. Chop the onion and garlic and drain the tomatoes.
2. Turn the machine to 'White Rice' setting and melt the coconut oil.
3. Add the onion and cook for 2 minutes.
4. Mix in the garlic and 2 tablespoons curry powder and continue to cook for another 2 minutes.
5. Cancel the 'White Rice' function to reduce heat and stir in the tomatoes, tomato sauce, chicken broth, and sugar.
6. Poke holes in the chicken and season with salt, pepper, and remaining curry powder.
7. Seal the pot and cook on 'White Rice' setting for 10 minutes then allow the pressure to release naturally.
8. Transfer the chicken to a bowl and shred it.
9. Return the chicken to the pot and return the pot to 'White Rice' setting.
10. Stir continuously for about 3 minutes.
11. Turn the pot to 'Keep Warm' function and pour in the coconut milk and allow to cook for another 10 minutes before serving.

Calories: 676 Sodium: 626 mg, Dietary Fiber: 4.9g Fat: 35.6g, Carbs: 20g, Protein: 69.7g.

Braised Chicken
with Sweet Tomatillos

Great tasting chicken with a light flavor from tomatillos.

Serves: 6
Prep Time: 10 Minutes
Cook Time: 4 Hours

- 2 tablespoons olive oil
- Salt and pepper to taste
- 3 1/2 pounds assorted chicken pieces
- 1 yellow onion
- 2 cups chicken broth
- 6 cloves garlic
- 1 1/2 pounds tomatillos
- 3 tablespoons cilantro
- 2 teaspoons ground cumin
- 1 tablespoon lime juice

1. Remove the husks from the tomatillos and wash them.
2. Mince the garlic and chop the onion and cilantro.
3. Turn the pot to 'White Rice' setting and add the olive oil.
4. Add the onion and cumin and cook for about 5 minutes.
5. Add the garlic and tomatillos and continue cooking until the tomatillos begin to soften.
6. Add the remaining ingredients to the pot and stir to ensure the chicken is coated.
7. Switch the pot to the 'Steamer' function and cook on low for 4 hours.

Calories: 608 Sodium: 486 mg, Dietary Fiber: 2.7g Fat: 26.1g, Carbs: 10.6g, Protein: 79.8g.

Green Salsa Chicken

A simple recipe to spice up your chicken that can be eaten by itself or used in tacos.

Serves: 4
Prep Time: 2 Minutes
Cook Time: 20 Minutes

1 tablespoon olive oil
4 boneless, skinless chicken breasts
1 teaspoon salt
1 teaspoon ground cumin
1 teaspoon garlic powder
1 teaspoon smoked paprika
1/2 teaspoon ground black pepper
1 16-ounce jar salsa verde

1. Place the oil in the pot and then add the chicken.
2. Sprinkle the salt, pepper, and spices over the chicken.
3. Pour the salsa into the pot making sure to evenly coat the chicken.
4. Seal the pot and cook on 'White Rice' setting for 10 minutes, then allow the pressure to release naturally for 10 minutes.
5. Transfer the chicken to a bowl and shred before serving.

Nutrition

Calories: 342 Sodium: 1359 mg, Dietary Fiber: 0.9g Fat: 14.8g, Carbs: 6.1g, Protein: 44g.

Spiced
Chicken Wraps

This is a simple recipe that brings the flavor of the middle east into your home.

Serves: 4
Prep Time: 5 Minutes
Cook Time: 10 Minutes

1 pound boneless, skinless chicken thighs
3 teaspoons olive oil
2 teaspoons dried oregano
1 teaspoon ground cumin
1 teaspoon ground cinnamon
1 teaspoon ground coriander
1 teaspoon salt
1/2 teaspoon ground allspice
1/2 teaspoon cayenne
1/2 cup water
4 large lettuce leaves
1 cup Tzatziki sauce

1. Cut the chicken into bite sized pieces.
2. Add the oil, spices, salt, and pepper to a Ziploc bag.
3. Put the chicken in the bag and shake well until the chicken is completely coated.
4. Turn the pot to 'White Rice' setting and add the remaining oil.
5. Add the chicken to the pot and cook for about 4 minutes, stirring occasionally.
6. Add the water and seal the lid.
7. Cook on 'White Rice' setting for 10 minutes then manually Allow the pressure to release naturally.
8. Wrap the chicken in lettuce leaves and top with Tzatziki sauce to serve.

Calories: 367 Sodium: 741 mg, Dietary Fiber: 5.6g Fat: 14.5g, Carbs: 24.6g, Protein: 36.5g.

Easy Enchilada Bowl

Bowls like this are growing in popularity thanks to their great flavor profile and low carb nature.

Serves: 4
Prep Time: 20 minutes
Cook Time: 35 minutes

2 tablespoons coconut oil

1 pound of boneless, skinless chicken thighs

3/4 cup red enchilada sauce

1/4 cup water

1/4 white onion

4 ounce can diced green chiles

1 fresh Jalapeño

1 cup shredded Mexican cheese

1. Turn the pot to 'White Rice' setting and melt the coconut oil.
2. Add the chicken and brown it on both sides.
3. Chop the onion, slice the jalapeño, and drain the chiles.
4. Add the onion, chiles, water, and enchilada sauce to the pot.
5. Turn the pot to the 'Meat/Stew' setting and cook for 25 minutes.
6. Transfer the chicken to a bowl and shred, then return to the pot.
7. Mix the chicken into the pot then turn the pot to 'Keep Warm' and continue cooking for another 10 minutes.
8. Top with cheese and jalapeños and serve.

Nutrition

Calories: 328 Sodium: 555 mg, Dietary Fiber: 1.1g Fat: 18.3g, Carbs: 5.2g, Protein: 34.8g.

Lemon Chicken

Lemon and chicken have always been a great pairing and they just got even easier to combine.

Serves: 8
Prep Time: 8 Minutes
Cook Time: 20 Minutes

- 8 boneless, skinless chicken thighs
- Salt and pepper to taste
- 1/2 teaspoon garlic powder
- 1/2 teaspoon smoked paprika
- 2 tablespoons olive oil
- 3 tablespoons butter
- 1/2 small onion
- 4 cloves garlic
- Juice of 1 lemon
- 2 teaspoons Italian seasoning
- Zest of half a lemon
- 1/3 low Sodium chicken broth
- 2 tablespoons heavy cream

1. Turn the pot to 'White Rice' setting and add the oil.
2. Dice the onion and mince the garlic.
3. Add the chicken to the pot, brown on both sides, then remove and set aside.
4. Add the butter and cook the onion and garlic in the pot for a few minutes.
5. Add the lemon juice to the pot and scrape up any brown bits from the bottom of the pot.
6. Mix in the Italian seasoning, lemon zest and chicken broth, then return the chicken to the pot.
7. Seal the lid and cook on 'White Rice' setting for 7 minutes.
8. Allow the pressure to release naturally for 2 minutes, then release the rest of the pressure manually.
9. Remove the chicken and set it aside.
10. Add the cream to the pot and stir until well combined.
11. Turn the pot to 'White Rice' setting and stir until the sauce starts to bubble.
12. Mix the chicken back into the pot and turn the pot off.
13. For added flair serve with lemon wedges as garnish.

Calories: 370 Sodium: 162 mg, Dietary Fiber: 0.4g Fat: 20.4g, Carbs: 2.1g, Protein: 42.7g.

CHAPTER
8
Main Entrées
Beef and Pork

Hands Off
Beef Barbacoa

If you like a little spice in your food you will love this barbacoa beef.

Serves: 9
Prep Time: 10 Minutes
Cook Time: 1 Hour 5 Minutes

5 cloves garlic
1/2 white onion
2 tablespoons lime juice
4 tablespoons chipotles in adobo sauce
1 tablespoon ground cumin
1 tablespoon ground oregano
1/2 teaspoon ground cloves
1 cup water
3 pounds beef eye of round
2 1/2 teaspoons salt
Black pepper to taste
1 teaspoon oil
3 bay leaves

1. Place the garlic, onion, lime juice, oregano, cumin, chipotles, cloves, and water in a blender and blend until smooth.
2. Turn the pot to 'White Rice' setting and add the oil.
3. Cut the steak into 3-inch pieces and add it to the pot, continue to cook until browned.
4. Pour the sauce into the pot, add the bay leaves and seal, then cook on 'White Rice' setting for 1 hour.
5. Allow the pressure to release naturally and transfer the meat to the bowl and shred.
6. Remove the bay leaves, then return he meat to the pot and stir before serving.

Nutrition

Calories: 289 Sodium: 766 mg, Dietary Fiber: 0.8g Fat: 9g, Carbs: 5.3g, Protein: 44.5g.

Balsamic Vinegar
Pot Roast

Pot roasts are awesome because they are so tasty and take little hands-on time.

Serves: 10
Prep Time: 10 Minutes
Cook Time: 50 Minutes

3 pounds boneless chuck roast
1 tablespoon kosher salt
1 teaspoon black pepper
1 teaspoon garlic powder
1/4 cup of balsamic vinegar
2 cups water
1/2 onion
1/4 teaspoon xanthan gum

1. Chop the onion and season the roast with salt, pepper, and garlic powder.
2. Turn the pot to 'White Rice' setting and brown the roast on all sides.
3. Add the vinegar, water, and onion to the pot and seal.
4. Cook on 'White Rice' setting for 40 minutes then allow the pressure to release naturally.
5. Remove the roast from the pot and set aside.
6. Return the pot to 'White Rice' setting and mix in the xanthan gum.
7. Return the roast to the pot and simmer for 10 minutes.
8. Remove from heat and serve.

Calories: 458 Sodium: 866 mg, Dietary Fiber: 2.7g Fat: 32.4g, Carbs: 3.4g, Protein: 37.7g.

Southwest
Steak Bowl

Bowls like this are popping up in restaurants all over the country thanks to their wonderful flavor profile and healthier nature.

Serves: 4
Prep Time: 5 Minutes
Cook Time: 15 Minutes

2 pounds of fajita steak strips
1 tablespoon of water
1 teaspoon garlic
1 tablespoon of olive oil
2 teaspoons of lime juice
1/2 teaspoon chili powder
1/2 teaspoon salt
1/2 teaspoon pepper
1 teaspoon of Cholula
3 Avocados

1. Mince the garlic and dice the avocado.
2. Turn the pot to 'White Rice' setting and add the olive oil.
3. Add the garlic and cook for a few minutes.
4. Add the remaining ingredients except for the avocado to the pot and stir to mix.
5. Seal the pot and cook on 'White Rice' setting for 10 minutes.
6. Allow the pressure to release naturally and turn the pot back to 'White Rice' setting.
7. Mix the ingredients to break up the meat into smaller pieces.
8. Continue stirring until the liquid reduces by half.
9. Top with avocado and serve.

Calories: 605 Sodium: 364 mg, Dietary Fiber: 10.4g Fat: 39.5g, Carbs: 15.4g, Protein: 50.2g.

Mocha Spiced
Pot Roast

This recipe gives off a bittersweet and smoky flavor that is incomparable.

Serves: 4
Prep Time: 10 Minutes
Cook Time: 50 Minutes

- 2 tablespoons finely ground coffee
- 2 tablespoons smoked paprika
- 1 tablespoon black pepper
- 1 tablespoon cocoa powder
- 1 teaspoon Aleppo pepper
- 1 teaspoon chili powder
- 1 teaspoon ground ginger
- 1 teaspoon sea salt
- 2 pounds beef chuck roast
- 1 cup brewed coffee
- 1 cup beef broth
- 1 small onion
- 6 dried figs
- 3 tablespoons balsamic vinegar

1. Chop the onion and figs and cut the roast into 2-inch cubes.
2. In a small bowl mix together the first 8 ingredients to create the rub.
3. Put the roast cubes in a large bowl and add 4 tablespoons of the rub and toss to coat.
4. Add the vinegar, figs, onions, broth, and coffee to a blender and blend until smooth.
5. Place the beef in pot and top with the sauce.
6. Seal the lid and turn the pot to the 'Meat/Stew' setting.
7. When the timer is done the pot will automatically turn to 'Keep Warm', allow the pressure to release naturally.
8. Serve with extra sauce.

Calories: 934 Sodium: 817 mg, Dietary Fiber: 5.6g Fat: 64.6g, Carbs: 24.5g, Protein: 62.7g.

Comfort
Cube Steak

Fantastic comfort food taste without the carbs that usually come with comfort food.

Serves: 6
Prep Time: 10 Minutes
Cook Time: 30 Minutes

2 pounds cube steak
1/3 cup flour
2 tablespoons oil
2 cups beef broth
2 onions
1 can cream of celery soup
1 dry package of onion soup mix

1. Cut the steak into smaller pieces.
2. Place the flour in a sealable bag then add the beef and toss to coat.
3. Turn the pot to 'White Rice' setting and add the oil.
4. Add the cube steak to the oil and brown on all sides then remove and set aside.
5. Add 3 tablespoons of beef broth to the pot and scrape the bottom of the pot to scrape up any brown bits.
6. Add the onions to the pot and cook on 'White Rice' setting for about 3 minutes.
7. Return the beef to the pot.
8. Mix the remaining ingredient together in a bowl and pour them over the steak.
9. Set to 'Brown Rice' and cook for 20 minutes.
10. Allow the pressure to release naturally and allow the mixture to cool for 5 minutes before serving.

Calories: 430 Sodium: 709 mg, Dietary Fiber: 1.3g Fat: 14.9g, Carbs: 12.6g, Protein:58g.

Beef
Stuffed Peppers

You won't believe how easy it is to put together these amazing single serve dishes.

Serves: 6
Prep Time: 5 Minutes
Cook Time: 15 Minutes

1 pound ground beef
1 can diced tomatoes and green chiles
1/4 white onion
1 teaspoon salt
1 teaspoon chili powder
1 teaspoon cumin
6 green bell peppers

1. Turn the pot to 'White Rice' setting and add the beef.
2. Brown the beef, breaking it into small bits.
3. Cut the peppers in half and dice the onion.
4. Mix the tomatoes, onion, salt, cumin, and chili powder into the beef.
5. Spoon the mixture into the pepper halves and set aside.
6. Rinse the pot out and return it to the machine.
7. Place the steam tray in the pot with one cup of water and place the peppers on the steam tray.
8. Seal and cook on 'White Rice' setting for 4 minutes.
9. Allow the pressure to release naturally and serve.

Calories: 183 Sodium: 445 mg, Dietary Fiber:1.9g Fat: 5.2g, Carbs: 9.8g, Protein: 24.3g.

Low-Carb Meatballs

These meatballs can be served over your favorite pasta substitute or eaten as is.

Serves: 5
Prep Time: 10 Minutes
Cook Time: 10 Minutes

- 1 1/2 pounds ground beef
- 3/4 cup grated parmesan cheese
- 1/2 cup almond flour
- 2 eggs
- 1 teaspoon salt
- 1/4 teaspoon black pepper
- 1/4 teaspoon garlic powder
- 1 teaspoon dried onion flakes
- 1/4 teaspoon dried oregano
- 1/3 cup warm water
- 1 teaspoons olive oil
- 3 cups sugar free marinara sauce

1. Combine all of the ingredients except for the last 2 into a large bowl and combine using your hands.
2. Roll the mixture into about 15 balls.
3. Turn the pot to 'White Rice' setting and add the oil.
4. Add the balls to the pot and brown on all sides.
5. Pour the marinara over the balls and seal the pot.
6. Cook on steam for 10 minutes then manually allow the pressure to release naturally.

Calories: 432 Sodium: 1234 mg, Dietary Fiber: 4g Fat: 16.1g, Carbs: 21.4g, Protein:47.6g.

Buttery
Roast Beef

This low carb recipe will almost literally melt in your mouth.

Serves: 6
Prep Time: 10 Minutes
Cook Time: 1 Hour

- **3 pounds beef roast**
- **1 tablespoon olive oil**
- **2 tablespoons ranch dressing seasoning mix**
- **1 jar pepper rings**
- **2 tablespoons zesty Italian seasoning mix**
- **8 tablespoons butter**
- **1 cup water**

1. Drain the pepper rings and reserve 1/4 cup of juice.
2. Turn the pot to 'White Rice' setting and add the oil.
3. Add the roast and brown on all sides.
4. Pour in the remaining ingredients except for butter over the roast.
5. Lay the butter on top of the roast and seal the pot.
6. Cook on 'White Rice' setting for 1 hour then allow the pressure to release naturally.

Calories: 589 Sodium: 569 mg, Dietary Fiber:0.3g Fat: 31.8g, Carbs: 2.3g, Protein: 69g.

Lime and Chile
Short Ribs

Keto or not this is a recipe you are going to be craving.

Serves: 4
Prep Time: 10 minutes
Cook Time: 40 Minutes

3 pounds beef short ribs
1 tablespoon chili powder
1 tablespoon cumin
1 teaspoon onion powder
1 teaspoon dried oregano
1 1/2 teaspoons salt
1/2 teaspoon pepper
1/2 teaspoon coriander
1/4 teaspoon cayenne pepper
4 cloves garlic
Juice and zest of 2 limes
2 tablespoons coconut oil
1/3 cup apple cider vinegar

1. Cut the ribs so there is one bone per section and mince the garlic.
2. Mix together the chili powder, cumin, onion powder, oregano, sea salt, black pepper, coriander, cayenne, garlic cloves, and lime zest in a small bowl.
3. Lay the ribs flat and sprinkle the spice mix over each section.
4. Turn the pot to 'White Rice' setting and melt the coconut oil.
5. Add the ribs and brown on both sides.
6. Press cancel and pour in the lime juice and vinegar.
7. Seal the pot and turn it to the 'Meat/Stew' setting and cook for 35 minutes.

Calories: 780 Sodium: 1100 mg, Dietary Fiber:1.2g Fat: 38.2g, Carbs: 3.8g, Protein: 99.1g.

Hawaiian
Pork Roast

A sweet and savory pork roast that takes a few ingredients and little hands on time.

Serves: 6
Prep Time: 5 Minutes
Cook Time: 8 Hours

2 red peppers
2 cups fresh pineapple
1 can full fat organic coconut milk
1 green onion
1 tablespoon dried basil
1 tablespoon dried oregano
1 teaspoon salt
3 pound pork shoulder roast

1. Dice the peppers and pineapple and mince the onion.
2. Add all of the ingredients to the pot and cover.
3. Turn to 'Steamer' mode and cook for 7 hours.
4. Shred the pork, then turn to 'Keep Warm' and cook for another hour.

Calories: 637 Sodium: 542 mg, Dietary Fiber:1.4g Fat: 48.2g, Carbs: 9.4g, Protein: 39g.

Quick and Easy Pork Tenderloin

This is a basic recipe spiced up by a keto friendly sauce that makes all the difference.

Serves: 3
Prep Time: 5 Minutes
Cook Time: 15 Minutes

1 pork tenderloin
1/2 onion
1/2 cup water
1 tablespoon olive oil
Salt and pepper to taste
1/2 cup heavy whipping cream
1/4 cup finely grated parmesan cheese
1 tablespoon Dijon mustard

1. Cut the pork loin in half width-wise and season with salt and pepper.
2. Turn the pot to 'White Rice' setting and add the oil.
3. Brown the loin on all sides then remove and set aside.
4. Slice the onion into thin slices then add it to the pot and cook for a few minutes.
5. Add the water to the pot and scrape up the brown bits from the bottom of the pot.
6. Return the loin to the pot and seal it.
7. Cook on 'White Rice' setting for 4 minutes then allow the pressure to release naturally.
8. Transfer the pork to a cutting board and let it rest.
9. Turn the pot back to 'White Rice' setting and add the cream and mustard.
10. Bring the sauce to a boil and allow it to boil for about 10 minutes.
11. Stir in the parmesan until it's melted.
12. Slice the pork and top with the sauce.

Calories: 120 Sodium: 69 mg, Dietary Fiber:0.6g Fat: 12.3g, Carbs: 2.6g, Protein: 0.8g.

Ribs in White BBQ

A delightful change to boring and sugar filled BBQ ribs.

Serves: 6
Prep Time: 5 Minutes
Cook Time: 45 Minutes

- **1 cup of water**
- **1/4 cup + 2 tablespoons apple cider vinegar**
- **3 pound rack of spare ribs**
- **1/2 teaspoon garlic powder**
- **1/2 teaspoon onion powder**
- **Salt and pepper to taste**
- **2 cans full-fat coconut milk**
- **2 tablespoons apple cider vinegar**
- **2 tablespoons lemon juice**
- **2 tablespoons whole grain mustard**
- **4 cloves garlic**
- **1 teaspoon honey**

1. Mince the garlic and set aside.
2. Place the steam rack in the pot and add the water and a cup of vinegar inside.
3. Pat the ribs dry and season with salt, pepper, onion powder, and garlic powder.
4. Place the ribs in the pot vertically and seal the pot.
5. Cook on 'White Rice' setting for 25 minutes.
6. Place the coconut milk in a skillet over medium heat.
7. When the milk begins to boil reduce to low heat and allow to simmer for 15 minutes.
8. Stir in the garlic, honey, lemon juice, remaining vinegar, and mustard, and remove from heat.
9. Preheat the broiler of your oven.
10. Remove the ribs from the pot and lay on a baking sheet curved side down.
11. Brush the ribs with the BBQ sauce then broil for 5 minutes.

Calories: 610 Sodium: 492 mg, Dietary Fiber: 1.3g Fat: 48.9g, Carbs: 3.8g, Protein: 35.1g.

Shredded
Pork

Enjoy with low-carb wraps or just eat as is.

Serves: 8
Prep Time: 30 Minutes
Cook Time: 35 Minutes

3 pounds pork shoulder
2 tablespoons tapioca starch
2 teaspoons garlic powder
2 teaspoons cumin
1 teaspoon coriander
1 teaspoon sea salt
3 tablespoons coconut oil
1 jar salsa verde
1/2 cup lime juice

1. Cut pork into 2-inch slices.
2. Turn the pot to 'White Rice' setting and melt the coconut oil.
3. Mix the remaining ingredients except for the salsa and lime juice.
4. Press each pork slice into the spice mix to coat well.
5. Brown each slice on both sides in the coconut oil.
6. Place all of the pork in the pot and cover in salsa verde and lime juice.
7. Turn the machine to the 'Meat/Stew' setting and cook for 35 minutes.
8. Manually allow the pressure to release naturally.
9. Turn the machine back to 'White Rice' setting and shred the pork.
10. Allow to continue to simmer until the liquid has reduced by half at least.

Calories: 554 Sodium: 372 mg, Dietary Fiber: 0.2g Fat: 41.6g, Carbs: 3g, Protein: 39.9g.

Tropical Island
Pork

An easy hands-off recipe that only takes a few ingredients to make the perfect pork dish.

Serves: 8
Prep Time: 10 Minutes
Cook Time: 1 Hour 30 Minutes

5 pounds boneless pork butt
1 tablespoon Hawaiian sea salt
1 teaspoon smoked paprika
1 cup water
1 green cabbage

1. Cut the pork into big chunks.
2. Mix the sea salt and paprika together and roll the pork chunks in the mixture.
3. Add the pork and water to the pot and cook on 'White Rice' setting for 1 hour and 30 minutes.
4. Allow the pressure to release naturally and remove the pork.
5. Slice the cabbage and place it in the pot.
6. Seal the pot and cook on 'White Rice' setting for 3 minutes.
7. Manually allow the pressure to release naturally and return the pork to the pot and mix well.

Nutrition

Calories: 570 Sodium: 896 mg, Dietary Fiber: 2.3g Fat: 19g, Carbs: 5.3g, Protein: 89.4g.

Cuban Pork

This citrusy pork dances over your tongue and doesn't need much to accompany it.

Serves: 10
Prep Time: 1 Hr 20 Minutes
Cook Time: 1 Hr 20 Minutes

8 cloves garlic

Juice of 1 grapefruit

Finely grated zest and juice of 1 lime

3 tablespoons olive oil

2 tablespoons light brown sugar

1 tablespoon fresh oregano leaves

2 teaspoons ground cumin

1 1/2 tablespoons salt

1 5-pound boneless pork shoulder

1 bay leaf

1. Quarter the pork shoulder.
2. Combine the garlic, grapefruit juice, lime zest and juice, 2 tablespoons of the oil, brown sugar, oregano, cumin, and salt in a blender and blend until smooth.
3. Transfer the marinade to a large bowl, and the pork and bay leaf, and refrigerate for 1 hour.
4. Turn the pot to 'White Rice' setting and add the remaining oil.
5. Remove the pork from the marinade and brown on all sides.
6. When the pork is browned add the marinade to the pot.
7. Turn the pot to 'White Rice' setting and cook for 1 hour 20 minutes.
8. Remove the pork and bay leaf and set the pork aside.
9. Turn the pot back to 'White Rice' setting and continue cooking until the sauce begins to thicken.
10. Shred the pork and mix it back into the pot before serving.

Calories: 378 Sodium: 1177 mg, Dietary Fiber: 0.5g Fat: 12.3g, Carbs: 4.2g, Protein: 59.7g.

CHAPTER 9

Main Dishes

Seafood

Seafood Gumbo

Enjoy a taste of New Orleans with this tasty gumbo.

Serves: 8
Prep Time: 10 Minutes
Cook Time: 10 Minutes

24 ounces sea bass fillets
3 tablespoons ghee
3 tablespoons Cajun seasoning
2 yellow onions
2 bell peppers
4 celery ribs
28 ounces diced tomatoes
1/4 cup tomato paste
3 bay leaves
1 1/2 cups bone broth
2 pounds medium raw shrimp, deveined

1. Pat the fish dry and cut into 2 inch cubes.
2. Chop the onions, peppers, and celery.
3. Season the fish with salt, pepper, and half of the Cajun seasoning.
4. Turn the pot to 'White Rice' setting and add the ghee.
5. Add the fish and cook for about 4 minutes flipping a few times to make sure it's evenly cooked.
6. Remove the fish with a slotted spoon and set aside.
7. Add the pepper, onions, celery, and remaining Cajun seasoning and cook for another few minutes.
8. Return the fish to the pot and add the tomatoes, paste, broth, and bay leaves.
9. Seal the pot and set it to 'White Rice' setting for 5 minutes.
10. Allow the pressure to release naturally and turn the pot back to 'White Rice' setting.
11. Add the shrimp and cook for 4 minutes.
12. Season with more salt and pepper to taste before serving.

Nutrition

Calories: 1254 Sodium: 5097 mg, Dietary Fiber: 2.6g Fat: 77.4g, Carbs: 31.3g, Protein: 106.1g.

Chunky Fish Chowder

A wholesome and filling meal that only takes a few minutes to make.

Serves: 4
Prep Time: 10 Minutes
Cook Time: 5 Minutes

- 3/4 cup chopped bacon
- 1 shallot
- 2 ribs celery
- 1 carrot
- 2 cloves garlic
- 3 Yukon Gold potatoes
- 4 cups vegetable broth
- 2 tablespoons butter
- 1 pound frozen wild caught Haddock fillets
- 1 cup frozen corn
- White pepper to taste
- 2 cups heavy cream
- 1 tablespoon potato starch

1. Chop the vegetables and bacon and mince the garlic.
2. Peel and cube the potatoes into small cubes.
3. Turn the pot to 'White Rice' setting and melt the butter.
4. Add the bacon and cook until browned.
5. Add the veggies and continue to cook until the vegetables begin to soften.
6. Add the fish, corn, and broth to the pot and seal the pot.
7. Select 'Brown Rice' setting and cook for 5 minutes.
8. Allow the pressure to release naturally and turn the machine to the 'Keep Warm' function.
9. Mix the starch and cream in a small bowl then stir it into the pot.
10. Allow the mixture to thicken for a few minutes before serving.

Calories: 790 Sodium: 1524 mg, Dietary Fiber: 3.8g Fat: 41g, Carbs: 58.7g, Protein: 46.8g

Shrimp Scampi

Perfect, buttery, shrimp scampi in your Aroma.

Serves: 6
Prep Time: 5 Minutes
Cook Time: 10 Minutes

2 tablespoons butter
1 pound frozen shrimp
4 cloves garlic
1/2 teaspoons red pepper flakes
1/2 teaspoons paprika
1 cup chicken broth
1/2 cup half and half
1/2 cup parmesan cheese
Pepper to taste

1. Mince the garlic.
2. Turn the pot to 'White Rice' setting and add the butter.
3. Add the garlic and red pepper and cook for 2 minutes.
4. Add the paprika, shrimp, broth, and pepper.
5. Cook on 'White Rice' setting for 2 minutes then manually allow the pressure to release naturally.
6. Turn the pot back to 'White Rice' setting then stir in the half and half and parmesan until the parmesan is completely melted.

Nutrition

Calories: 151 Sodium: 277 mg, Dietary Fiber: 0.2g Fat: 7.8g, Carbs: 2.6g, Protein: 17.1g

Steamed Crab Legs

Perfectly steamed crab legs in less than 10 minutes.

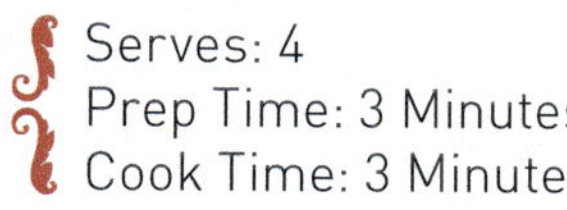

Serves: 4
Prep Time: 3 Minutes
Cook Time: 3 Minutes

2 pounds wild-caught Snow Crab legs

1 cup water

1/3 cup ghee

Lemon slices

1. Place the steam tray in the pot with 1 cup water
2. Put the legs in the pot and seal the lid.
3. Set to the 'Steam' setting for 3 minutes then allow the pressure to release naturally.
4. Melt the ghee in a microwave or on the stovetop.
5. Serve the legs with ghee and lemon slices.

Calories: 417 Sodium: 1736 mg, Dietary Fiber: 0.1g Fat: 21g, Carbs: 0.2g, Protein: 53.4g

Lemon and Dill
Salmon

Salmon can be a little strong but the lemon and dill take the edge off.

Serves: 4
Prep Time: 5 Minutes
Cook Time: 10 Minutes

1 lb. salmon fillet

Salt and pepper to taste

1/4 cup + 3 teaspoons lemon juice

3 teaspoons fresh dill

1. Chop the dill and cut the salmon into thirds.
2. Add a cup of water, 1/4 lemon juice, and a steam rack in the pot.
3. Place the salmon on the rack skin side down and season with salt and pepper.
4. Drizzle the remaining lemon juice over the salmon and sprinkle with dill.
5. Seal the pot and turn to the 'Steam' function for 2 minutes.
6. Allow the steam to release naturally before opening.

Calories: 152 Sodium: 52 mg, Dietary Fiber: 0.1g Fat: 7g, Carbs: 0.4g, Protein: 22.2g

Coconut Milk Shrimp

A protein packed and tasty meal to get you through your day.

Serves: 4
Prep Time: 10 Minutes
Cook Time: 10 Minutes

1 pound shrimp shelled, deveined

1 tablespoon ginger

1 tablespoon garlic

1/2 teaspoon turmeric

1 teaspoon salt

1/2 teaspoon cayenne pepper

1 teaspoon garam masala

1/2 can unsweetened coconut milk

1. Mince the ginger and garlic.
2. Mix all the ingredients in a casserole dish.
3. Put a steam tray in the pot with two cups of water and put the dish on the steam tray.
4. Cover the dish with foil and seal the pot.
5. Turn the pot to 'Steam' and cook for 4 minutes.
6. Allow the pressure to release naturally and serve with extra coconut milk if desired.

Nutrition

Calories: 99 Sodium: 708 mg, Dietary Fiber: 1g Fat: 7.6g, Carbs: 3.6g, Protein: 5.5g

Alaskan Cod
with Olives and Fennel

Cod is great by itself but the fennel and olives help round out the flavor.

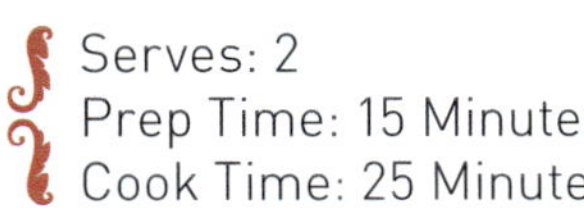

Serves: 2
Prep Time: 15 Minutes
Cook Time: 25 Minutes

2 tablespoons olive oil
1/2 white onion
1 head garlic
1 1/2 cups chicken broth
1/4 cup olive brine
1/4 cup canned tomato purée
Salt and pepper to taste
1/2 cup green olives
1 head fennel
One 12-ounce Alaskan cod fillet
1/4 bunch basil

1. Cut the garlic head in half and cod fillet into 3 inch squares.
2. Pit the olives and crush them then cut the fennel into quarters.
3. Turn the pot to 'White Rice' setting and add the oil.
4. Place the garlic and onion cut side down in the oil and cook for a few minutes.
5. When the garlic and onion start to brown flip them over and add the broth, olive brine and tomato purée to pot and turn it off.
6. Add the olives and fennel to the pot and season with salt and pepper.
7. Seal the pot and cook on 'Steam' setting for 10 minutes.
8. Manually allow the pressure to release naturally and remove the veggies with a slotted spoon and set aside.
9. Season the cod with salt and pepper and put it in the pot.
10. Seal the pot and cook the cod on steam for 4 minutes.
11. Remove the fish and transfer it to serving bowls.
12. Tear the basil leaves into the pot.
13. Top the fish with the vegetables then spoon the basil broth over the fish to serve.

Nutrition

Calories: 260 Sodium: 797 mg, Dietary Fiber: 2.1g Fat: 16.3g, Carbs: 8.4g, Protein: 19.9g

Fast Salmon Cakes

A quick, easy, and mouth-watering way to get fish into your diet.

Serves: 2
Prep Time: 5 Minutes
Cook Time: 5 Minutes

- 2 5 ounce pouches of pink salmon
- 1 egg
- 1/2 jalapeño
- 2 tablespoons light mayo
- 1/8 red onion
- 1/4 teaspoon garlic powder
- 1/4 teaspoon chili powder
- Salt and pepper to taste
- 1 tablespoon avocado oil

1. Mince the jalapeño and red onion.
2. Turn the pot to 'White Rice' setting and add the oil.
3. Mix the remaining ingredients in a bowl until they ingredients are well blended.
4. Form the mixture into 4 – 6 patties.
5. Place the patties in the pot and cook for about 5 minutes flipping halfway through to heat on both sides.

Calories: 260 Sodium: 797 mg, Dietary Fiber: 2.1g Fat: 16.3g, Carbs: 8.4g, Protein: 19.9g

Flaky
Fish Stew

This Mediterranean delight has a slight citrus note to compliment the fish.

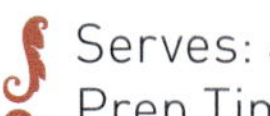

Serves: 4
Prep Time: 5 Minutes
Cook Time: 15 Minutes

- **4 tablespoons olive oil**
- **1 red onion**
- **4 cloves garlic**
- **1/2 cup dry white wine**
- **8 ounce bottle clam juice**
- **2 1/2 cups water**
- **1 can diced tomatoes**
- **Salt, pepper, and red pepper to taste**
- **2 pounds boneless, skinless sea bass fillets**
- **2 tablespoons fresh lemon juice**
- **2 tablespoons chopped fresh dill**

1. Cut the bass into 2 inch pieces.
2. Mince the garlic and thinly slice the onion.
3. Turn the pot to 'White Rice' setting and add 2 tablespoons of oil.
4. Add the onions and cook until they begin to soften.
5. Add the garlic and continue to cook for another minute.
6. Add the wine and scrape up any brown bits from the bottom of the pot.
7. Mix in the claim juice, tomatoes, salt, and peppers.
8. Seal the pot and cook on 'White Rice' setting for 5 minutes.
9. Manually allow the pressure to release naturally and return the pot to 'White Rice' setting.
10. Add the fish and continue to cook on 'White Rice' setting for about 5 minutes or until the fish is cooked.
11. Mix in the remaining oil, lemon juice, and dill before serving.

Calories: 477 Sodium: 454 mg, Dietary Fiber: 1.3g Fat: 20.1g, Carbs: 12.2g, Protein: 55g

White Clam
Sauce

This is a great seafood sauce that can be served over almost anything to offer a protein packed change of pace.

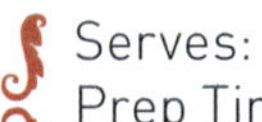
Serves: 4
Prep Time: 10 Minutes
Cook Time: 10 Minutes

1/4 cup butter
2 tablespoons olive oil
1 teaspoon salt
1/4 teaspoon black pepper
1 clove garlic
1/2 cup dry white wine
2 tablespoons lemon juice
2 pounds small clams
1 teaspoon grated lemon zest

1. Mince the garlic.
2. Turn the pot to 'White Rice' setting and add the butter, oil, salt, and pepper.
3. Add the garlic and cook for about 2 minutes.
4. Add the wine and lemon juice and cook for another 2 minutes.
5. Add the clams and cook for another 3 minutes or until they open, discarding any that don't open.
6. Press the cancel button to remove from heat and allow to rest a few minutes to thicken before serving.

Calories: 299 Sodium: 1487 mg, Dietary Fiber: 1g Fat: 19g, Carbs: 26.2g, Protein: 1.6g

Lime
Shrimp

Use these to top your favorite keto pasta or just pop them in your mouth by themselves.

Serves: 4
Prep Time: 5 Minutes
Cook Time: 5 Minutes

2 tablespoons butter
2 cloves garlic
1 cups bone broth
1 pound frozen shrimp
15 drops lime essential oil
Salt and pepper to taste
Cilantro to taste

1. Turn the pot to 'White Rice' setting and add the butter.
2. Mince the garlic and add it to the pot.
3. Add some salt and pepper and cook for a few minutes.
4. Add the broth, lime oil, and shrimp.
5. Set the pot to manual and cook on 'White Rice' setting for 5 minutes.
6. Chop the cilantro.
7. Allow the pressure to release naturally and sprinkle with cilantro before serving.

Calories: 196 Sodium: 249 mg, Dietary Fiber: 0g Fat:7.8g, Carbs: 1.5g, Protein: 28.3g

Tilapia
with Veggies

Tilapia has a unique flavor that doesn't need much to accompany it. These veggies help to round out the meal in a single pot.

Serves: 4
Prep Time: 15 Minutes
Cook Time: 5 Minutes

2 cups mushrooms
2 cups Tomatoes
2 cups Spinach
3/4 cups Basil
2 cloves garlic
3 tablespoons olive oil
1/4 cups lime juice
1/2 teaspoons zest of lime
1/4 teaspoons salt
1/2 teaspoons black pepper
1 pound Tilapia fillets

1. Dice the mushrooms, tomatoes, and spinach and mix them together in a bowl.
2. Place the remaining ingredients except for the Tilapia in a blender and blend until smooth.
3. Place the Tilapia in individual pieces of foil and cover each piece with the spice mixture.
4. Spread the vegetable mix evenly over each piece of tilapia.
5. Roll the foil edges over the fish to create a foil packet.
6. Place the packets on the steam tray.
7. Place the steam tray and 1 cup of water into the pot.
8. Seal and cook on 'White Rice' setting for 5 minutes.
9. Allow the pressure to release naturally and serve immediately.

Calories: 216 Sodium: 206 mg, Dietary Fiber: 1.9g Fat: 11.9g, Carbs: 6.2g, Protein: 23.7g

Basil Tilapia with Tomatoes

This is a fresh light meal perfect for a dinner on the porch.

Serves: 4
Prep Time: 5 Minutes
Cook Time: 5 Minutes

4 Tilapia fillets
Salt and pepper
3 Roma tomatoes
2 cloves garlic
1/4 cup basil
2 tablespoons olive oil
Salt and pepper to taste
Balsamic vinegar

1. Mince the garlic and chop the basil.
2. Season the fish with salt and pepper and place in a steamer basket.
3. Place the basket in the pot with 1/2 cup of water.
4. Seal the pot and cook the fish on 'White Rice' setting for 4 minutes.
5. Dice the tomatoes toss them in a bowl garlic, basil, olive oil, salt, pepper, and vinegar.
6. Allow the pressure to release naturally and transfer the fish to a serving plate.
7. Top with the tomato mixture and serve.

Nutrition

Calories: 173 Sodium: 45 mg, Dietary Fiber: 1.2g Fat: 8.2g, Carbs: 4.2g, Protein: 22g

Lobster Tails
with Butter Sauce

You can never, ever, go wrong with lobster tails.

Serves: 4
Prep Time: 5 Minutes
Cook Time: 5 Minutes

1 tablespoon old bay seasoning
4 Lobster Tails
1 cup butter
1 clove garlic
1/2 teaspoon salt
1/2 teaspoon pepper
2 teaspoons lemon juice
1 teaspoon dill weed

1. Mince the garlic.
2. Put 1 cup of water in the pot and mix in the old bay seasoning.
3. Put the lobster in the steamer basket and put the basket in the pot.
4. Seal the pot and cook on 'White Rice' setting for 4 minutes.
5. While the lobster cooks, heat 1 tablespoon of butter in a saucepan over medium heat until the butter starts to brown.
6. Add the remaining butter and garlic and cook for another minute.
7. Mix in the remaining ingredients and transfer the melted butter to a bowl for serving.
8. Allow the pressure to release naturally and serve the lobster with butter sauce.

Calories: 540 Sodium: 1803 mg, Dietary Fiber: 0.1g Fat: 47.3g, Carbs: 0.6g, Protein: 28.2g

CHAPTER

10

Dessert

Chinese Egg Custard

This simple Chinese dessert doesn't take a lot of ingredients, but it does leave an impression.

Serves: 4
Prep Time: 4 Minutes
Cook Time: 16 Minutes

3 Eggs
1 1/2 cups whole milk
1/4 teaspoon salt
4 tablespoons granulated sugar

1. Combine the sugar, 1 cup milk, and salt in the pot and set the machine to the 'Steamer' function.
2. Stir continuously until the sugar is dissolved into the milk.
3. Remove from heat and allow to cool before mixing in remaining milk.
4. Beat the eggs in a large glass measuring cup, then stir in the milk mixture.
5. Strain the mixture twice with a small strainer or cheesecloth.
6. Pour the mixture into 4 – 4-ounce ramekins and cover tightly with foil.
7. Rinse out the pot and add the steam tray and 1 cup of fresh water.
8. Place the ramekins on the steam tray and cook on 'Steam' for 10 minutes.
9. Allow the pressure to release naturally for 10 minutes before removing the ramekins.

Nutrition

Calories: 147 Sodium: 230 mg, Dietary Fiber: 0g Fat: 47.3g, Carbs: 16.4g, Protein: 7.1g

Chocolate Cheesecake

This cheesecake proves that you can have your cake and eat it too.

Serves: 8
Prep Time: 10 Minutes
Cook Time: 35 Minutes

- 1/4 cup almond flour
- 1/4 cup coconut flour
- 1 1/2 tablespoons low carb sweetener
- 2 tablespoons butter
- 16 ounces cream cheese
- 1/2 teaspoon stevia concentrated powder
- 1/2 teaspoon monk fruit powder
- 1/3 cup + 2 1/2 tablespoons unsweetened cocoa powder
- 1 egg
- 2 egg yolks
- 1/4 cup sour cream
- 3/4 cup heavy cream
- 6 ounces baking chocolate
- 1 teaspoon vanilla extract

1. Melt the butter in the microwave.
2. Cut parchment paper to size and put in a springform pan.
3. Mix together the flours, sweetener, 2 1/2 tablespoons cocoa powder, and butter in bowl then press the mixture into the pan.
4. Blend the cream cheese with the remaining cocoa powder and sweeteners.
5. Add the eggs and yolks and blend into the cream cheese.
6. Melt the chocolate chips and blend into the mix.
7. Blend in the remaining ingredients until smooth.
8. Pour the mix into the pan.
9. Place a steam tray in the pot with 1 cup of water and put the pan on the steam tray.
10. Cover the cake loosely with foil and seal the pot.
11. Cook on 'White Rice' setting for 20 minutes, then allow the pressure to release naturally for 15 minutes.
12. Refrigerate for a few hours before serving.

Calories: 529 Sodium: 258 mg, Dietary Fiber: 11.7g Fat: 42.2g, Carbs: 35.4g, Protein: 16.9g

Chocolate Mousse

A smooth and chocolatey treat guaranteed to satisfy your sweet tooth.

Serves: 5
Prep Time: 10 Minutes
Cook Time: 20 Minutes

4 egg yolks
1/2 cup sugar replacement
1/4 cup water
1/4 cup cacao
1 cup whipping cream
1/2 cup almond milk
1/2 teaspoon vanilla
1/2 teaspoon salt

1. Beat the egg yolks in a medium bowl.
2. Mix together the water, cacao, and sugar replacement in a saucepan.
3. Heat the pan over medium-low heat and mix in the milk and cream.
4. Add the salt and vanilla and mix well.
5. Remove from heat and mix the eggs into the mix.
6. Pour the mixture into ramekins.
7. Place the steam tray in the pot with 1 1/2 cups water.
8. Place the ramekins on top of the steam tray and seal the pot.
9. Cook on 'White Rice' setting for 6 minutes.
10. Allow the pressure to release naturally and transfer to the refrigerator for at least 4 hours before serving.

Calories: 180 Sodium: 251 mg, Dietary Fiber: 1.8g Fat: 17.6g, Carbs: 5g, Protein: 4g

Lemon Ricotta Cheesecake

Though it may sound unconventional, this cheesecake is quite delicious.

Serves: 6
Prep Time: 10 Minutes
Cook Time: 40 Minutes

8 oz cream cheese
1/4 cup sugar replacement
1/3 cup Ricotta cheese
Zest of one lemon
Lemon juice from one lemon
1/2 teaspoon Lemon Extract
2 eggs

1. Mix all the ingredients except for the eggs in a medium bowl.
2. Mix in the eggs until just incorporated.
3. Pour into a greased cake pan and cover with foil.
4. Place the pan on a steam tray and place the steam tray and 2 cups water into the pot.
5. Cook on 'White Rice' setting for 30 minutes, then allow the pressure to release naturally

Calories: 178 Sodium: 151 mg, Dietary Fiber: 0.3g Fat: 15.8g, Carbs: 3.1g, Protein: 6.4g

Crème
Brulee

Desserts don't get much easier to make, and you won't believe it's keto friendly.

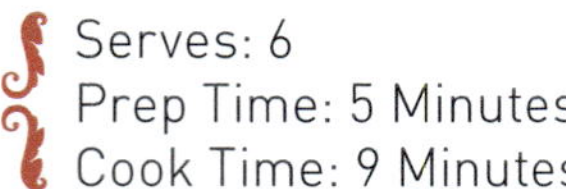

Serves: 6
Prep Time: 5 Minutes
Cook Time: 9 Minutes

2 cups heavy whipping cream
6 egg yolks
5 tablespoons sugar replacement
1 tablespoon vanilla extract

1. Beat the eggs in a bowl and mix in the cream and 3 tablespoons of sugar.
2. Pour the mixture into 6 small ramekins.
3. Cover the ramekins with foil and place 3 on a steam tray.
4. Cover the ramekins with a silicone steamer and add the other three ramekins on top.
5. Seal the pot and cook on 'White Rice' setting for 9 minutes.
6. Allow the pressure to release naturally for 15 minutes.
7. Transfer the ramekins to the fridge and allow them to cool for a few hours.
8. Sprinkle with the remaining sugar replacement before serving.

Nutrition

Calories: 198 Sodium: 24 mg, Dietary Fiber: 0g Fat: 19.3g, Carbs: 2g, Protein: 3.5g

Butter

This is a versatile sweet treat that can turn anything it tops into a dessert.

Serves: 10
Prep Time: 5 Minutes
Cook Time: 1 Hour 5 Minutes

3 pounds sweet red apples
2 large Golden Delicious apples
1 large Granny Smith apple
1/4 cup filtered water
3 large Medjool dates
1 teaspoon ground cinnamon
1/2 teaspoon ground cloves
1/4 teaspoon ground ginger
1/8 teaspoon ground nutmeg

1. Core and chop the apples and pit the dates.
2. Combine all of the ingredients in the pot and cook on 'White Rice' setting for 20 minutes.
3. Allow the pressure to release naturally then transfer the contents to a blender.
4. Blend until smooth and then transfer the mixture to a medium pot.
5. Cook on the stove over medium heat for another 40 minutes, stirring often.
6. Allow to cool before using.

Calories: 74 Sodium: 2 mg, Dietary Fiber: 3.1g Fat: 0.2g, Carbs: 19.4g, Protein: 0.3g

Apple Upside Down Cake
with Lavender

This recipe will calm both your sweet tooth and your soul at the same time.

Serves: 6
Prep Time: 10 Minutes
Cook Time: 25 Minutes

- 4 gala apples
- 2 tablespoons lemon juice
- 1/2 teaspoon dried lavender flowers
- 1/2 cup tigernut flour
- 1/3 cup cassava flour
- 2 tablespoons coconut flour
- 1/2 teaspoon baking powder
- 1/4 teaspoon fine sea salt
- 1/4 cup palm shortening
- 3 tablespoons maple syrup
- 1 teaspoon vanilla extract
- 1 tablespoon gelatin powder

1. Peel and slice the apples.
2. Line the bottom of a cake pan with parchment paper and place on the steam tray.
3. Mix the apples, lemon juice, and lavender together and pour into the cake pan.
4. Mix the tigernut flour, cassava flour, coconut flour, baking powder, salt in a large bowl.
5. In a separate bowl combine the shortening, syrup, and vanilla.
6. Add the gelatin powder to the shortening mix and stir well.
7. Pour the shortening mix into the flour mix and stir well until it forms a dough.
8. Transfer the dough to a piece of parchment paper and press down into a circle that will fit in the cake pan.
9. Place the dough over the apples in the cake pan and cover with foil.
10. Pour 2 cups of water in the pot and place the steam tray in the pot.
11. Cook on 'White Rice' setting for 25 minutes.
12. Allow the pressure to release naturally then turn the cake pan over to remove the cake.

Nutrition

Calories: 263 Sodium: 106 mg, Dietary Fiber: 6g Fat: 15.1g, Carbs: 28.8g, Protein: 2.3g

Chocolate Peanut Butter Cheesecake

One of everybody's favorite flavor combinations, and its keto friendly!

Serves: 8
Prep Time: 5 Minutes
Cook Time: 18 Minutes

16 ounces cream cheese

2 eggs

2 tablespoons powdered peanut butter

1 tablespoon cocoa

1 teaspoon vanilla extract

1/2 cup sugar replacement

1. Blend the cream cheese and eggs together in a medium bowl.
2. Combine the rest of the ingredients in the bowl.
3. Pour into 8-ounce mason jars and cover with foil.
4. Place the jars in the pot with a cup of water.
5. Cook on 'White Rice' setting for 18 minutes, then let the pressure release naturally.
6. Transfer the jars to the fridge and allow to cool for at least a few hours before serving.

Calories: 228 Sodium: 207 mg, Dietary Fiber: 0.8g Fat: 21.3g, Carbs: 3.5g, Protein: 7g

Dark Chocolate Cake
with Walnuts

A fluffy chocolate cake with crunchy walnuts for juxtaposition.

Serves: 6
Prep Time: 10 Minutes
Cook Time: 30 Minutes

- 1 cup almond flour
- 2/3 cup sugar replacement
- 1/4 cup unsweetened cocoa powder
- 1/4 cup chopped walnuts
- 1 teaspoon baking powder
- 3 eggs
- 1/3 cup heavy whipping cream
- 1/4 cup coconut oil

1. Mix the ingredients together in a bowl until they look fluffy.'
2. Pour the batter into a bundt pan that fits your pot.
3. Place the pan on a steam tray and put 2 cups of water and the steam tray in the pot.
4. Seal the pot and cook on 'White Rice' setting for 20 minutes.
5. Allow the pressure to release naturally for 10 minutes before opening.

Nutrition

Calories: 203 Sodium: 37 mg, Dietary Fiber: 2.2g Fat: 19.5g, Carbs: 4.7g, Protein: 5.9g

Sweet Coconut
Custard

This is a fun sweet treat that you will want to make all the time.

Serves: 4
Prep Time: 5 Minutes
Cook Time: 30 Minutes

1 cup unsweetened coconut milk
3 eggs
1/3 cup sugar replacement
4 drops pandan extract

1. Combine all of the ingredients and pour them into a casserole dish and cover with foil.
2. Add the steam tray and 2 cups of water to the pot.
3. Place the casserole dish on the steam tray and cook on 'White Rice' setting for 30 minutes.
4. Allow the pressure to release naturally then transfer to the fridge until the custard sets

Calories: 198 Sodium: 56 mg, Dietary Fiber: 1.4g Fat: 17.6g, Carbs: 4.4g, Protein: 5.5g

Pudding
Chocolate Cake

Chocolate pudding is good. Chocolate cake is great. Chocolate pudding cake is the best.

Serves: 6
Prep Time: 10 Minutes
Cook Time: 6 Minutes

2/3 cup dark chocolate
1/2 cup applesauce
2 eggs
1 tsp vanilla
1/4 teaspoon salt
1/4 cup arrowroot
3 tablespoons cocoa powder

1. Chop the chocolate into small pieces.
2. Place the steam tray in the pot and add 2 cups of water.
3. Place the chocolate in a casserole dish and turn the pot to 'White Rice' setting.
4. Melt the chocolate in the pot then remove the dish from the pot and press cancel.
5. In a medium bowl beat the eggs then mix in the apple sauce and vanilla.
6. Add the dry ingredients to the bowl and continue to mix until you can't see any dry spots.
7. Mix the bowl into the chocolate in the casserole dish and return the dish to the pot.
8. Seal the pot and cook on 'White Rice' setting for 4 minutes.
9. Allow the pressure to release naturally and serve.

Calories: 141 Sodium: 134 mg, Dietary Fiber: 1.7g Fat: 7.4g, Carbs: 15.7g, Protein: 4g

Blueberry
Mug Cake

It doesn't get any easier than this, and the whole family will love how it tastes.

Serves: 1
Prep Time: 5 Minutes
Cook Time: 10 Minutes

1/3 cup almond flour
1 egg
1 tablespoon maple syrup
1/2 teaspoon vanilla
1/8 teaspoon salt
1/2 cup blueberries

1. Combine all of the ingredients in a bowl.
2. Transfer to an 8 ounce mason jar and cover with foil.
3. Add the steam tray and a cup of water to the pot.
4. Place the jar on the steam tray and seal the pot.
5. Cook on 'White Rice' setting for 10 minutes.
6. Allow the pressure to release naturally and serve while still warm.

Calories: 387 Sodium: 368 mg, Dietary Fiber: 5.8g Fat: 22.4g, Carbs: 32.5g, Protein: 14.1g

Almond and Coconut Cake

This Keto-friendly cake skips the gluten too but still manages to be moist and delicious.

Serves: 8
Prep Time: 10 Minutes
Cook Time: 40 Minutes

- 1 cup almond flour
- 1/2 cup unsweetened shredded coconut
- 1/3 cup sugar replacement
- 1 teaspoon baking powder
- 1 teaspoon apple pie spice
- 2 eggs
- 1/4 cup butter
- 1/2 cup heavy whipping cream

1. Mix the dry ingredients in a medium bowl.
2. Mix the wet ingredients in the bowl one at a time.
3. Pour the mix into a greased cake pan and cover with foil.
4. Pour 2 cups of water into the pot.
5. Put the cake pan on the steam tray and lower the steam tray into the pan.
6. Seal the pot and cook on 'White Rice' setting for 40 minutes.
7. Allow the pressure to release naturally for 10 minutes.
8. Remove from the pot and allow to cool an additional 15 minutes before serving.

Calories: 160 Sodium: 64 mg, Dietary Fiber: 1.5g Fat: 15.3g, Carbs: 3.2g, Protein: 2.9g

Carrot
Cake

Fluffy carrot cake taste with a fraction of the carbs.

Serves: 8
Prep Time: 10 Minutes
Cook Time: 50 Minutes

3 eggs
1 cup almond flour
2/3 cup sugar replacement
1 teaspoon baking powder
1 1/2 teaspoons apple pie spice
1/4 cup coconut oil
1/2 cup heavy whipping cream
1 cup shredded carrots
1/2 cup chopped walnuts

1. Mix together all the ingredient with a hand whisk.
2. Grease a cake pan and pour the mixture into the pan.
3. Cover the pan with foil and place on the steam tray.
4. Add the steam tray to the pot with 2 cups of water.
5. Set on the 'Cake' setting for 40 minutes.
6. Allow the pressure to release naturally for 10 minutes.
7. Serve by itself or enjoy with a little icing.

Calories: 185 Sodium: 38 mg, Dietary Fiber: 1.3g Fat: 17.5g, Carbs: 3.7g, Protein: 5g

Pumpkin Spice
Pudding

A sweet and easy dessert perfect for the holidays.

Serves: 4
Prep Time: 2 Minutes
Cook Time: 6 Minutes

1 tablespoon vanilla
1 teaspoon pumpkin pie spice
2 eggs
1/4 cup Sugar
3 tablespoons cornstarch
15 ounce can pumpkin puree
12 ounce can evaporated milk

1. Beat the eggs in a medium bowl.
2. Mix in half the milk, the pumpkin puree, and the vanilla into the eggs and set aside.
3. Mix the sugar, spice, and starch together in the pot of your Aroma.
4. Turn the pot to 'White Rice' setting and slowly stir in the remaining milk to the pot.
5. Continue stirring on 'White Rice' setting for about 3 minutes.
6. Press the cancel button and mix in the pumpkin mix.
7. Turn the pot back to 'White Rice' setting and stir continuously for another 3 minutes.
8. Remove from heat and allow to cool before eating.

Calories: 387 Sodium: 140 mg, Dietary Fiber: 15.1g Fat: 8.7g, Carbs: 66.2g, Protein: 12.3g

Lemony Cheesecake

A slightly more complicated dessert but with that comes amazing guiltless flavor.

Serves: 8
Prep Time: 10 Minutes
Cook Time: 35 Minutes

- 3/4 cup almond flour
- 2/3 cup + 2 tablespoons powdered erythritol sweetener
- 1/8 teaspoon salt
- 2 tablespoons butter
- 1 pound cream cheese
- 1/4 cup lemon juice
- 1 teaspoon lemon zest
- 1 teaspoon lemon extract
- 2 eggs
- 2 tablespoon heavy whipping cream

1. Line a springform pan with parchment paper and set aside.
2. Melt the butter in a bowl and mix in the salt, flour, and sugar.
3. Press the crust into the pan and set aside.
4. Beat the cream cheese in medium bowl until smooth, then mix in the lemon juice, zest, and extract.
5. Beat in the eggs one at a time.
6. Beat in the cream then pour the mixture into the prepared crust.
7. Wrap the pan in foil and place it on the steam tray.
8. Pour 1 cup of water into the pot and lower the steam tray into the pot.
9. Seal and cook on 'White Rice' setting for 35 minutes.
10. Allow the pressure to release naturally then transfer the cake to the refrigerator for a few hours before serving.

Nutrition

Calories: 319 Sodium: 245 mg, Dietary Fiber: 1.2g Fat: 30.2g, Carbs: 4.2g, Protein: 8.1g

Chocolate Vanilla
Pudding Cake

Make this chocolate cake now and enjoy it later.

Serves: 6
Prep Time: 15 Minutes
Cook Time: 3 Hours

- 3/4 cup butter
- 2 ounces unsweetened chocolate
- 1/2 cup heavy cream
- 2 tablespoons instant coffee crystals
- 1 teaspoon vanilla extract
- 4 tablespoons unsweetened cocoa powder
- 1/3 cup almond flour
- 1/8 teaspoons salt
- 5 eggs
- 2/3 cup sugar replacement

1. Turn the pot to 'White Rice' setting and add the butter and chocolate.
2. Stir continuously until melted then remove from heat.
3. In one small bowl mix together the heavy cream, coffee crystals, and vanilla.
4. In a separate small bowl mix the cocoa, flour, and salt.
5. In a third small bowl beat the eggs then mix in the sugar replacement.
6. Mix the eggs into the pot.
7. Add the cocoa mix stirring continuously.
8. Add in the cream mix stirring continuously until and even batter forms.
9. Close the lid and turn to 'Steam' on low for 3 hours.

Calories: 386 Sodium: 274 mg, Dietary Fiber: 3.6g Fat: 38.7g, Carbs: 7.2g, Protein: 8.3g

UMAMI *Fifth flavor*

Often called the “fifth flavor” after sweet, salty, sour, and bitter, umami can best be described as savory, but what does savory taste like? In Japanese, umami translates to “a pleasant savory taste.” Scientifically, umami is determined by the amount of glutamate in a particular food. (Think of it as a natural way of getting a flavor boost similar to MSG). The amazing thing about umami is that it can be found in all kinds of foods. Try adding a pinch of one of these ingredients to almost any recipe. **Often the taste is amazing!**

Vegetables/Plants

- Seaweed (kombu and nori)
- Soybean products (Soy sauce, miso, tofu)
- Tomatoes
- Green teas
- Kimchi (Korean fermented vegetables)
- Mushrooms

Meats

- Bacon
- Ham
- Pork
- Beef
- Chicken
- Eggs

Seafood

- Sardines
- Bonito (Dried fish flakes)
- Tuna
- Mackerel
- Shrimp
- Anchovies
- Oysters
- Mussels
- Caviar and other fish eggs

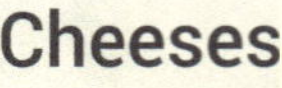

Cheeses

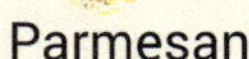

Parmesan

Comte/Gruyere

Roquefort

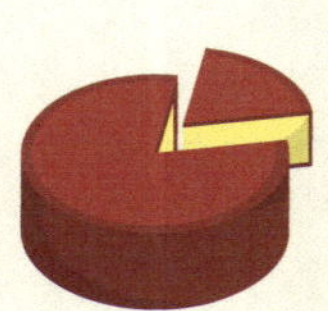

Gouda

Cheddar

Flavor Building

The best way to start building flavors is with a general seasoning with salt and black pepper. You can also experiment with these herbs and spices to build fun, new flavors with different proteins.

BEEF	SALMON	PORK	CHICKEN	VEGETABLES
Shallots	Lemon Pepper	Mustard	Rosemary	Olive Oil
Garlic	Citrus	Thyme	Garlic	Thyme
Thyme	Paprika	White Wine	White Wine	Mint
Cumin	Dill	Apple Cider	Thyme	Onion Powder
Rosemary	Basil	Rosemary	Soy Sauce	
Red Wine	Olive Oil		Lemon Pepper	
			Olive Oil	

Wine and Beer Pairing

Try these varieties with your favorite meats and fish.

NEW YORK OR RIBEYE STEAKS

Wine	Beer
Cabernet Sauvignon	IPA
Malbec	Brown Ale
Shiraz	Stout

SALMON

Wine	Beer
Sauvignon Blanc	Pilsner
Pinot Grigio	Lager
Riesling	IPA

PORK

Wine	Beer
Chardonnay	Brown Ale
Pinot Noir	IPA
	Stout

WHITE FISHES

Wine	Beer
Sauvignon Blanc	Light Ale
Chardonnay	Pilsner
	Hefeweissen

CHICKEN

Wine	Beer
Sauvignon Blanc	Pilsner
Merlot	Lager
Pinot Noir	Light Ale

10 CLASSIC *Salad Dressings*

Ranch

-  mayonnaise
-  buttermilk
-  chives
-  dill
-  onion powder
-  garlic powder
-  salt
-  black pepper

Caesar

-  canola oil
-   parmesan cheese
- anchovy
-  fresh garlic
-  egg yolk
-  black pepper

Bleu Cheese

-  blue cheese
-  buttermilk
-  sour cream
-  mayonnaise
-  white wine vinegar
-  sugar
-  garlic powder
-  black pepper

Thousand Islands

-  mayonnaise
-   ketchup
-  white vinegar
-  sugar
-    sweet pickle relish
-  salt
-  black pepper

Italian

-  olive oil
-  white or red wine vinegar
-   garlic powder
-   oregano
-   dried basil
-  onion powder
-  crushed red pepper
-  salt
-  black pepper
-  lemon juice

Balsamic Vinaigrette

-  balsamic vinegar
-  honey
-  dijon mustard
-  olive oil
-  garlic
-  salt
-  black pepper

Honey Mustard

-   dijon mustard
-  honey
-  apple cider vinegar
-  salt
-  vegetable oil

Greek

-  red wine vinegar
-  olive oil
-  lemon juice
-  dried oregano
-  salt
-  black pepper

French

-  vegetable oil
-  ketchup
- sugar
-  white vinegar
-  water
-  garlic powder
-  salt
- black pepper

Russian

-  onion
- mayonnaise
-   ketchup
- horseradish
-   hot sauce
- 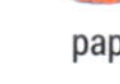 worcestershire sauce
-  paprika
-  salt

10 CLASSIC *Sauces*

 Bordelaise	 red wine ·  shallots ·  dried thyme ·  bay leaf ·  beef stock ·  salt ·  black pepper
Hollandaise	 egg yolks ·  lemon juice · butter · salt
 Mayonnaise	 egg yolks ·  dry mustard ·  sugar ·  lemon juice ·  white wine vinegar ·  vegetable oil ·  salt
Buffalo	 Hot sauce (like Frank's Red Hot) ·  butter · vinegar · Worcestershire sauce ·  garlic powder
Italian Tomato	 tomatoes ·   onions ·  garlic ·   olive oil ·  basil ·   oregano ·  salt ·  black pepper
Chimichurri	 fresh parsley ·  garlic ·  oregano ·  olive oil ·  white wine vinegar ·  salt ·  black pepper
Salsa Verde	 tomatillos ·  onion ·  serrano chile ·  garlic ·  cilantro ·  vegetable oil ·  salt
Alfredo	 butter ·  heavy cream ·  garlic ·  Parmesan cheese ·  parsley
Bechamel	 milk ·  butter ·  flour · salt
 Barbecue	  ketchup ·  apple juice ·  apple cider vinegar ·   brown sugar ·  butter ·   chili powder ·  garlic ·  onion ·   salt

A FUNCTIONAL PANTRY:

If you are going to cook a wide variety of dishes, you will need to have certain ingredients on-hand at all times. Keep your pantry well stocked with these ingredients:

All-purpose flour: Good for general baking and other kitchen uses

Baking powder: A double acting leavening agent that is needed for most baking

Baking soda: A leavening agent that is used when there are acidic ingredients

Kosher salt: less harsh tasting than table salt and good for cooking

Black pepper: used for seasoning before and after cooking

Olive oil: flavorful and good for low-temperature cooking and salad dressings

Vinegars: white, apple cider, white wine, red wine, and balsamic

Baking chocolate: good for a variety of desserts

Vanilla extract: flavorful addition to baked goods

White sugar: needed for most types of baking

Brown sugar: needed for many types of cakes, cookies, as well as savory dishes

Honey: a great natural sweetener

Long grain white rice: great as a light side dish

Brown rice: a healthier alternative to white rice

Breadcrumbs: handy for baking and frying

Stocks: chicken, beef, and vegetable for sauces, stews, and additional flavor

Beans: high in protein and fiber and useful in many dishes

Dry herbs and spices: bay leaves, cayenne pepper, chili powder, cinnamon, cloves, crushed red pepper, cumin, curry powder, fennel seed, garlic, ginger, nutmeg, oregano, paprika (sweet and smoked), rosemary, thyme

Dairy: milk, salted and unsalted butter, eggs, plain yogurt

Cheeses: cheddar, Parmesan, goat cheese, low moisture mozzarella

HOW TO CHOOSE VEGETABLES:

Leafy greens

Look for greens that are green all over. Otherwise, they may be starting to rot.

Tomatoes

Avoid bruised or discolored tomatoes. Tomatoes sold on the vine typically last longer than those sold without the vine.

Potatoes

Avoid potatoes that have a slight greenish hue. Look for potatoes that do not have any deep scars or large bruises.

Carrots

Look for carrots that have a healthy orange color and fresh-looking greens.

Peppers

Peppers should be free from bruises and their skin should be smooth and not wrinkly. Also look for healthy looking stems.

Mushrooms

Look for firm, fresh, smooth appearance. If the cap is closed underneath the flavor will be delicate. If it is open and you can see the gills it will have richer flavor. Fresh herbs: Herbs will last longer if they have the roots attached. After buying fresh herbs, put them in a glass of water to help them stay fresh longer.

HOW TO CHOOSE MEATS:

Beef

Most beef is either "choice" or "prime." Prime has the highest fat content, but it is also very expensive. If you can afford prime, it's the best, but most choice beef is quite good as well. When shopping for beef, look for marbling (the more the better) and try to find beef that has a healthy red color.

Grain fed or grass fed?
Most beef in the United States is grain fed, and this is what Americans are used to eating. Grass fed beef has a stronger flavor and often a higher fat content. A lot of grass-fed beef is grain fed and then finished on grass.

Chicken

When buying chicken, it's all about freshness. Fresh chicken should have very little smell and the skin should be a healthy yellowish color. Commercial chicken is often pre-brined, meaning it has been injected with salt water. While brining a chicken before cooking is a great way to improve flavor and moisture, avoid pre-brined chicken because you will end up paying for water. Also avoid chicken raised with any kind of hormones. When selecting a whole chicken, try to find one that is between four and five pounds for best flavor and texture.

Pork

Pork comes in many varieties, and again, freshness is key. Pork chops should be a light pink color with small ribbons of fat through the meat. Always look for well-marbled pork. When buying pork loins and tenderloins, look for pieces that have been well trimmed. Otherwise, you end up paying for fat you will throw away. When buying bacon, avoid those containing a lot of sugar in the dry rub.

Fresh fish

Fresh fish—meaning it has not been frozen—is always better. It will have a better texture and fresher flavor. When buying salmon, look for fish with high fat content. This will make the meat juicier. Also, make sure your salmon has a sweet smell and not a fishy smell. Ahi tuna should be deep red in color and should have almost no smell at all. Also, look for well-trimmed tuna that has had the bloodline removed. White fishes like flounder, halibut, cod, and sole should have a slightly sweet smell and slick, not dry, looking flesh.

Shellfish

Avoid buying frozen shellfish. It will have a mushy texture and slightly sulfurous smell. When buying oysters, try to buy local because oysters are sold live. For lobsters and crabs, live-bought is best. Otherwise, they can have a fishy smell. Pre-cooked lobsters and crab often become overcooked when reheated.

WAYS TO COOK *Vegetables*

ASPARAGUS		
Steam	Roast at	Grill
10 min	350 - 10 min	5 min

CARROTS		
Steam	Roast at	Grill
15 min	350 - 20 min	10 min

POTATOES		
Steam	Roast at	Grill
20 min	350 - 40 min	15 min

ZUCCHINI		
Steam	Roast at	Grill
10 min	350 - 20 min	10 min

BELL PEPPERS		
Steam	Roast at	Grill
5 min	350 - 10 min	5 min

GREEN BEANS		
Steam	Roast at	Grill
5 min	350 - 15 min	Do not grill

BROCCOLI		
Steam	Roast at	Grill
10 min	350 - 15 min	10 min

CAULIFLOWER		
Steam	Roast at	Grill
10 min	350 - 15 min	10 min

WAYS TO COOK *Meat*

NY STEAK/RIBEYE	
Broil	Grill
4 min per side	4 min per side

FILET MIGNON	
Broil	Grill
5 min per side	5-6 min per side

TRI TIP	
Roast at	Grill
375 - 40 min	25-30 min

CHICKEN (WHOLE)	
Roast at	Grill
375 - 90 min	90 min

CHICKEN (BREAST)	
Sautee	Grill
8 min per side	5-6 min per side

CHICKEN (THIGHS)	
Roast at	Grill
375 - 30 min	15-20 min

PORK CHOPS	
Sautee	Grill
5 min per side	5 min per side

PORK TENDERLOIN	
Roast at	Grill
350 - 20 min	12-15 min

HOW LONG DOES FOOD LAST IN THE FREEZER? (RAW UNLESS STATED OTHERWISE)

Meat, poultry, eggs & seafood

Beef/Lamb/Pork	4 to 12 months
Ham (cooked)	1 to 2 months
Ham	6 months
Chicken/turkey	9 months
Eggs	DO NOT FREEZE EGGS
Chicken nuggets	1 to 3 months
Hamburger patties	3 to 4 months
Hot dogs	1 to 2 months
Lean fish	6 months
Fatty fish	2 to 3 months
Shellfish	3 to 6 months

Produce

Fruit (except bananas)	10 to 12 months
Bananas	3 months
Citrus fruit	4 to 6 months
Most vegetables	8 to 10 months
Tomatoes	2 months

Dairy

Ice Cream	1 to 2 months
Butter	6 to 9 months

Other

Soup/stew	2 to 3 months
Fruit juice	8 to 12 months
Cake	4 to 6 months
Cookies (baked)	3 months
Cookie dough	2 months
Pies (baked)	2 to 4 months
Pies (unbaked)	8 months

KITCHEN UNIT CONVERSION

1 teaspoon	=	1/3 tbsp	=	4.9 ml
1 dessertspoon	=	2 tsp	=	9.9 ml
1 tablespoon	=	1.5 dstsp 3 tsp	=	14.8 ml
1 fuid ounce	=	2 tbsp 6 tsp	=	29.6 ml
1 cup	=	16 tbsp 48 tsp	=	236.6 ml
1 quart	=	4 cup	=	946 ml
1 gal	=	4 quart 16 cup	=	3.79 l
1 ounce	=	2 tbsp	=	28.4 g
1 pounds	=	16 oz	=	453.6 g

Made in the USA
Columbia, SC
03 July 2025

60256132R00087